Free-Range Kids

Growing up in the Forties and Fifties

Free-Range Kids

©Barbara Knight 2019

Cover illustration by Ryan Curtis, photography by Barbara Knight

Proofing and typesetting: Ryan Curtis and Julia Knight

Published by: Sculptural Images

Printed by: Ingram Spark

All rights reserved. No part of this publication may be reproduced, stored in a retrieval system or transmitted in any form or by any means, electronic mechanical, photocopying, recording or otherwise, without the prior permission of the publishers.

Dedication

This book is dedicated to brother Bernard who was too young to share these free-ranging years and sister Jane who did.

Early Memories

My first clear memory is of waking in a strange large white room in a bed with bars all around it. I don't think I was all that frightened, but I was puzzled. There were two other beds like mine in the room, and I could see other kids asleep in them. I climbed over the top of the bars and landed rather heavily on a slippery, shiny floor. Thus began my life as a free-range kid.

Just as I was scrambling to my feet a lady, who I didn't know, came and scooped me up and deposited me back into the cage-like bed. She pulled the blanket up over me and said, 'Naughty little girl. You aren't allowed out. Now just be good and I'll bring you your breakfast.'

I sat there, wondering what I had done that was naughty. I also began wondering where I was, and why I was in this place. Where were Mummy and Daddy and my sisters, and why had I been put in here? I don't remember crying, but I think I must have been fairly upset.

The next thing to happen was another strange lady came to my bed carrying a tray. She put the tray on a little table that she pulled across my bed. Then she started trying to spoon porridge into my mouth. I felt quite indignant about this for I had been feeding myself for as long as I could remember, so I turned my head away.

'Come on dear,' she said in a cajoling voice. 'You have to eat or you won't get better.'

Incensed I said with all the dignity a not quite three year old could muster, 'I feed self.'

There ensued a battle of wills in which she tried to force the porridge between my firmly clenched teeth. She finally gave in and let me feed myself.

After she left me in peace I finished the porridge and drank a glass of juice, then sat there wondering what to do with the tray. Ages later the lady returned and said, 'Good little girl,' and took the tray away.

Before she left I asked, 'Why am I here?'

She put down the tray again and sat next to my bed and said, 'You're in hospital because you're a sick little girl. When your Mummy and Daddy brought you in last night you had a very high temperature and a bad rash. You have to stay here until you get better. Now try to get some sleep.'

I'd just woken up and didn't feel like going to sleep again, so I climbed out of bed once more and peered up at the girl in the next bed. She was sleeping so I walked over to the other bed where a boy was lying very still. He had his eyes open so I knew he was awake, but when I talked to him he just stared at me. I thought he must be too young to understand what I was saying, so I wandered further across the room.

There was a big open door leading to an outside area and I went through it. It led to a long verandah where two big girls were lying on beds with wheels. They both had long wavy hair and nice faces. They smiled at me and one said, 'Look who's here. What's your name little girl?'

'My name is Barbara, what's yours?'

They both laughed and one said, 'I'm Audrey and this is Gloria.' I was thinking this could be the beginning of a nice, friendly talk when Gloria said, 'Where did you sprout from?'

I didn't quite know how to answer this because I didn't know what sprout meant, so I just stood there.

Suddenly the lady who had brought my breakfast came dashing out through the door

'You naughty little girl,' she said, as she swooped me up into her arms. 'You're not allowed out of bed. I was so worried when I couldn't find you.'

She plonked me back in the cage bed and said, 'Don't you do that again. You're a sick little girl and must stay in bed and rest.'

I didn't feel the least bit sick, although I did feel a bit itchy. I lay back and pulled up my nightie and I could see that I had a rash on my tummy and legs. I thought this must be why they were saying I was sick, but I couldn't see why it meant I had to stay in bed.

I lay back down and tried to remember how I'd got to this place. The lady said Mummy and Daddy had brought me here, but I couldn't remember. I just hoped they'd come back soon and take me home.

I think I must have slept for a while because the next thing I knew there was another lady with a tray. There were some sandwiches and ice cream and jelly on the tray and this lady smiled nicely and said, 'I hear you like to feed yourself, so I'll leave you to it.'

After I finished everything on the tray this lady returned and said, 'Good girl. Now settle down and have a nice afternoon nap.'

I thought she must have been joking. I'd already had a morning nap and I never had both. I waited until she left the room and again climbed out of bed. Once more I headed out through the door to see the nice big girls Audrey and Gloria. I thought they'd be pleased to see me, because they had seemed so friendly before but Audrey said, 'I think you're too sick to be out of bed little one. One of the nurses will be after you'.

I was about to say that I didn't feel sick when an angry looking lady, who I now knew must be a nurse, hurried towards me, lifted me up rather roughly and carried me back to bed under her arm. This nurse lady was not very tall but she was so wide she looked almost square, and she was quite frightening.

'Now you stay there, or we'll have to strap you in.'

I didn't like the sound of this, even though I wasn't sure what she meant about strapping me in. I closed my eyes and thought of my Mummy and my sisters and my little baby brother. This made me feel sad and I had a little cry. I'd been told big girls weren't supposed to cry so I didn't let anyone see me.

Later that day the nice nurse came and lifted me out of the cage bed and said, 'Your Mummy's come to visit. Let's put on your dressing gown and I'll take you out.'

I was taken through a long corridor until we came to a big room. The floor of this room was covered with shiny linoleum, and across what looked like an enormous expanse stood Mummy. She was dressed in a tweed coat and wore a hat that I rather liked because it had a feather in it. I went to run to her, but the lady who I thought was nice held me firmly and said, 'You can't go. You're infectious and could give your germs to your Mummy.'

I felt like crying, but Mummy knelt down on the other side of the room and said, 'It won't be for long Baby. Soon we'll be able to take you home. And I've brought you some lollies and a book.'

She threw the book and some paper wrapped lollies across the floor and I eagerly gathered them up. I watched as Mummy straightened up. Was she leaving already?

'Be a good girl,' she said. 'I'll be back tomorrow and will bring you a surprise.'

As she disappeared through the door on the other side of the room I started to cry, even though people could see me. It didn't seem fair that I'd been put in this place and I wasn't even sick. I yelled, 'I want to go home.'

The nice nurse cuddled me and said, 'It won't be long before you can. Now let's take you back to bed and I'll read you your new book.'

The next day was much the same as the first. I'd climb out of bed and be put back with threats of strapping me in, but this didn't deter me. There wasn't anything to do in bed and I didn't feel sick enough to want to sleep.

In the afternoon Mummy came again, and this time she had a lovely surprise. It was a beautiful kewpie doll on a stick. My biggest sister had been bought one of these at the Hobart Show the previous year and I had badly wanted one too. The doll had a little round face and big blue eyes with long eyelashes. She was dressed in a pink lace ballerina's dress and had tiny pink shoes that you could take off. Straight away I loved her to bits, and spent the remainder of the afternoon happily in my cage because I had her to play with. That night I put her to sleep next to me on the pillow and didn't feel as lonely.

The next day I couldn't wait for breakfast to be over so that the nurses would leave the room and I could go and show Audrey and Gloria my new doll. I climbed out of bed and headed for the open door, but before I could reach the big girls the square nurse grabbed me.

'OK Miss, You've had your last chance. Now I'm going to strap you in.'

She held me roughly under one arm while she went to a cupboard and brought out a thing that had straps and buckles like I'd seen on shoes. After putting me into the bed she tied the strap things around my waist and then buckled them onto the bars of my bed. I felt very uncomfortable and began to cry, but all she said was, 'That'll teach you,' and left the room.

Not even having my kewpie doll for company could cheer me up, and I sat miserably in my bed all morning. The nice nurse undid the straps for me to eat my lunch, but said I'd have to have them on again until the evening.

When Mummy visited I wanted to tell her about the nurse strapping me into bed, but it was the cross square one that came to take me to see her and I was a bit frightened of that one. I did shout across the room, 'I not sick Mummy. I want to go home.'

Mummy said she'd talk to the doctor about letting me come home.

The next morning the cross nurse came to see me as I was finishing my breakfast. She said that I could go home but first I had to be disinfected. I wasn't sure what this big word meant, but I soon found out. That nasty square nurse put me in the hottest, smelliest bath you can imagine. Something strange had been put in the bath that made my eyes ache and my nose run, and the water was so hot I was sure it would scald me and leave burn marks all over my body. I hadn't liked that nurse from the start, but now I hated her.

But worse was to come. When I went to pick up my kewpie doll from the bedside table she grabbed it away from me and said, 'You can't take that from here. It will have too many germs on it.'

I couldn't believe what I was hearing. I thought she must have been saying that to be mean to me because I'd climbed out of bed so often. As soon as I saw Mummy standing across the room I ran into her open arms.

In between sobs I spluttered out, 'That mean nurse won't give me my dolly. Make her give it to me Mummy.'

I was sure she would tell the mean nurse off and get me my doll, but instead she said, 'I'm afraid if the nurse says so, dolly has to stay here. But don't worry Darling. I'll buy you another one next year at the show.'

I felt so disappointed I wouldn't even hold Mummy's hand while we walked out to the car. She should have stood up to the nasty square nurse.

When we reached the car Daddy said, 'Let the little one sit in the front with me.'

He put his arm around me and I snuggled into his side, while Mummy sat in the back with my two older sisters and the baby. It certainly made me feel loved and important to be sitting in the front with Daddy, and I was glad Mummy sat in the back because I was still cross with her for not getting my dolly back for me. Strangely enough, the loss of my kewpie doll was the most traumatic thing about that sojourn in hospital.

Years later I asked Mum what hospital had I been in and why had I been put in there. She told me I had been in Vaucluse Hospital. It was the only public hospital for patients with infectious diseases, and had begun operations during the polio epidemic of 1938. I would have been there two years later. I also asked her why I'd been taken there because as far as I could remember I hadn't felt sick. Mum told me the doctor had diagnosed me as having scarlet fever, which was highly contagious and very serious in the days before antibiotics were available. I have since wondered if I was wrongly diagnosed for I really don't think I was there for very long, but unfortunately my mother is no longer around to verify this.

A few years later I contracted whooping cough, another infectious disease, but this time I was quarantined in my parents' bedroom. The main things I remember about that illness are hanging out the bedroom window to watch for the daily arrival of the doctor and the very strange noise I made when I coughed.

At the time my brother John would have been about three and my other brother Roger a toddler so it must have been a worry for Mum to have a child with such a highly infectious disease in the house. In hindsight it is surprising that she kept me at home instead of packing me off to hospital again. Perhaps she realised how traumatic my previous hospitalisation had been.

Although I know my memories of my brief but traumatic stay in hospital are truly mine, I'm not sure about some of the others.

An incident that occurred when I was about four seems very clear to me, but it was reinforced by retelling for it became part of family folklore. It concerned me and a hat.

We were all going somewhere that required being dressed up; perhaps it was to my brother Roger's christening for in those days women and girls all wore hats to church. Mum helped us all on with our coats and then our hats. My hat was made of blue felt and had a row of felt flowers around the brim. For some reason I loathed that hat, so I took it off and said I wasn't wearing it. Mum tried to talk me into putting it back on, but when I refused Dad stepped in. He told everyone else to go to the car and when we were alone he said, 'Put it on or you'll stay here by yourself.'

I thought anything would be preferable to wearing that hat so refused to do as I was told. Dad repeated his threat and I still refused, so he moved towards the door saying, 'You're going to be very lonely here by yourself.'

I still refused to do as he said so he walked towards the front door. As I watched him move away did I believe he'd leave? Did I really think I'd be all right alone in the house? The only thing I remember clearly was being determined that I wasn't going anywhere in that hat.

When Dad reached the door he turned around and said, 'Are you going to put it on?'

After I still refused he came back, grabbed my hand tightly and said, 'God you're a stubborn little one,' and pulled me out to the car.

My sisters moved over and made room for me on the seat and everyone in the car was very quiet. At the time they were quite shocked at me standing up to Dad, but later they laughed about how I'd looked with my red, determined face and the hat crushed under my arm.

There are photos of me when I was very young having a tea party with my two older sisters, Shirl and Jane. I think I remember this happening, but my memories may be of later ones when I was older. I clearly remember making tea from dock leaves and gathering flowers from the garden to be used as cakes.

We had a toy tea set with a teapot, cups and saucers and plates. Shirl poured the tea, because she was the oldest, while Jane and I spread the flowers out on the tiny plates. I know we drank the tea and ate the flowers and pretended to be grownup ladies. I consider this game to be responsible for what has become a life-long habit with me, for I taste flowers and leaves with gay abandon, although I'm a little more circumspect with regard to berries. It amuses me how frequently flowers are now used to decorate demonstration dishes on Master Chef, for I have been doing this for years.

One of our favourite games was schools. I think we began playing this once Jane started real school. Shirl had stopped playing imaginary games with us by then, and the brothers were too young to join in, so we had the tall grasses that grew in the back yard as our pupils. We both insisted on being a teacher, so we divided the grasses between us and strode between the rows pretending they were children sitting in desks.

Jane said all teachers had canes so of course we equipped ourselves with thin twitchy sticks. When the wind blew and moved the grasses we lay into them with our sticks, berating our imaginary pupils for being fidgety and not sitting still. We were really vicious, angry teachers.

In calmer moments we made ink out of some lovely black berries that grew on a plant that scrambled along a side fence. This plant fascinated us for it had strange grey-white foliage that was almost as soft as cottonwool and looked a bit like little animal faces. When these fell off the berries appeared, and we crushed them up and mixed them with a little water until we had something that was the consistency of ink. Sometimes Mum gave us scraps of paper to write on, but paper was scarce during the War Years so more often we wrote on pieces of bark or pretended the fence was a blackboard and wrote on that.

Free-Range Kids

For a long time Jane and I believed in fairies, and were firmly convinced that some of them lived under our house. The house was built on a hill so there was a space underneath where you could stand up, which then sloped away until it was very low. There were foundation posts towards the front of the house and wire between the posts. We'd crawl up as far as we could go and peer through the wire. There must have been ventilation grates at the sides of the house because light filtered into this dark space. We watched the dust motes floating through the air and told ourselves these were fairies.

One year one of us was given a small metal stove as a Christmas present. We loved this stove, and made cakes from mud that we decorated with flowers and then baked in the oven. After a few days of playing with it we decided, for some strange reason, to give it to the fairies. We crawled up to the posts, lifted the wire and pushed the stove under as far as we could, then sat back to watch the fairies enjoy our present. Nothing happened, so we thought they might be shy with us watching. We crawled back out, leaving our treasure for them to use.

The next day we returned. The stove was still in the same place, looking forlorn and dusty. Obviously our present had not been appreciated so we decided to take it back. Unfortunately this proved to be impossible. No matter how we leaned against the wire and stretched our fingers we couldn't reach the stove.

Eventually we gave up trying to retrieve it and left it there. Sometimes we'd crawl up to the wire and look at it. As it slowly rusted away in the dirt so too did our belief in fairies.

Barbara Knight

My Family

I was born in 1937, the third child in a family of seven. Ours was a very happy home because Mum was unfailingly calm and loving and had the knack of making each of us feel very special. She told us often what good children we were, so we tried to live up to her expectations. Dad wasn't around that much because he taught night school two or three nights a week and umpired during the football season, but when he was at home he was a fairly easy-going sort of a Dad.

Mum and Dad first met when he started at Moonah School. She had already been there a year. Previously she had attended a little private school run by two spinster sisters. When she'd learnt all they had to teach her Mum begged to be allowed to go to the state school. Dad had grown up in the town of Burnie and when his family moved to Lutana, a suburb of Hobart, he went to Moonah School for his grade six year. At the time he was about twelve and Mum a year older. Her memories of him at the time was that he was a very neat, rosy-cheeked little boy and very clever. She used to tell us proudly that he came top of the class at the end of the year. Dad didn't seem to remember Mum from that time, which I think is sad.

I have a copy of a photo taken of their grade six class. In it Dad does indeed look a neat, rosy-cheeked boy and is grinning cheekily. Mum has a pretty little face, long dark hair and looks very serious.

They met again when they were eighteen and nineteen at a party at Lenton, the beautiful old house where Mum grew up.

Her father had bought twelve acres of land in Derwent Park and named the lovely house he had built on it after the village of Lenton where his father had been born. It was quite a grand house with a double gable roof and a verandah across the front and along the two sides. My grandfather Gordon Pell came to Tasmania in 1870, when he was twenty-one and by the time he was fifty had this property, which he farmed. He must have also had investments for Mum spoke fondly of what she called quarter days, which were the days dividends were paid on these investments. The whole family would go to town on quarter days, have lunch at a restaurant and buy new clothes.

Granddad Pell and Nan met when Nan's father, who was a solicitor, did some work for him. At the time of their meeting she was thirty and he fifty-five, although the marriage certificate gives Nan's age as twenty-nine. When I noticed this I wondered why my dear little Nan had lied about her age, particularly as she was marrying a much older man. Perhaps in those days a woman was considered on the shelf once she turned thirty. Anyhow despite this minor deception and the twenty-five year age gap they fell in love, and had a very happy marriage until his death at seventy-six.

From what Mum and Auntie Ron told us about their father he was a remarkably hands-on dad for the times. He bathed them and often cooked their meals thus freeing his young intellectual wife to attend art classes and literary meetings. Mum said her happiest childhood memories were of riding on her father's shoulders through the orchard and being up early with him to milk the cow.

He died when Mum was seventeen but seemed to have left Nan well-provided for. She lived comfortably during her long years of widowhood, and for most of the time also provided a home for Mum's sisters. Barb returned home when she was widowed and Ron when she separated from her first husband. They also both continued to live with Nan when they married their second husbands.

From the time I remember they all lived together at Tower Road, along with our two cousins, Chris and Des. Lenton was rented out and I used to wonder why we couldn't live in that beautiful house. After all it belonged to our Nan and she didn't seem to want to be there. It was many years before I learnt that the house in Tower Road had been bought with money left to Mum in a trust fund, and that Nan had needed the rent from Lenton to continue to keep all her dependants.

Mum and Dad met at a party at Lenton. During the Depression Years there wasn't much entertainment around for young people and few of them had much money. Nan evidently kept open house, and welcomed all her children's friends for evenings of dancing to the piano, games and supper. Dad came with a friend of one of her sisters, and I think my parents fell in love when Dad kissed Mum during a game of spin the bottle.

Neither of the mothers approved of the match, Grandma because she didn't think Mary would make a suitable wife for a workingman, and Nan thought Bernie Knight a bit too working class. They had certainly been brought up very differently.

Nan thought young ladies shouldn't have to work and Auntie Barb and Auntie Ron went along happily with this idea and never even attempted to find employment. Mum, however, did want to be part of the workforce and spoke fondly of her times of working, first in a small library and later in a book store and a furniture shop. She said it was hard to keep a job during the Depression Years because businesses were doing it tough. Because of this I don't think her periods of employment were very extensive, and she would have liked to work more, even though her mother said it was unnecessary.

In contrast, Dad began an apprenticeship at the Zinc Works as soon as he finished second year high school. At the end of that year students sat the Proficiency Exam and many young people left school at this stage. From the time he began earning a wage he was expected to hand his earnings over to Grandma, who then gave him back sufficient for his train fares, lunches and a little spending money. I'm not sure how long he put up with this, but eventually he must have insisted on a more equitable share of his earnings, for he bought Mum a very pretty little diamond ring when they became engaged.

Despite Nan's initial concerns about her daughter's choice of a beau Dad won her around when he spent an afternoon sketching with her and did a remarkably good drawing of Lenton. He was actually very talented, but never had the time or interest in developing his talent. I have a slightly damaged landscape that he did in sepia tones that is very good, and one of my sisters has two oil painting he did, one of fishermen and the other a landscape, but not much else remains. For a long time Mum kept the drawing of Lenton but it seems to have disappeared when she died.

During the Depression Years workers had their pay cut, and Dad was helping his mother with house payments. Because of this Mum and Dad went together for seven years before they could afford to marry. After such a long time both mothers were resigned to the marriage. They should have been happy with the way it turned out, for our parents were together for fifty years, and they created a happy home for us seven kids.

There can't have been much money around, for soon we were a large family and Dad was only a boilermaker/welder at the Zinc Works. He did earn extra money umpiring and teaching at night school and Mum was a good money manager so we always had plenty of food and clothes, a reasonably nice house by the standards of the day and Dad always had a car, quite a rarity in those days. From the time I was about seven we also had a shack where we spent every school holiday.

Our house was fairly similar to most of the others in our street. There was a verandah at the front, and this was where Mum did our hair on school days and where we played when it rained. Inside the front door was a long passage, and it was another place to play when it was too cold and wet to be outside. Mum would take up the long runner that went the length of the passage and we'd help her put polish on the linoleum. Then we'd put on our thickest socks and skate up and down the passage, imagining we were on skating rink. This was a lot of fun and also achieved a nice shiny floor.

There were three bedrooms down the left side of the passage and a little box room at the end. On the right were the front room, or parlour, and the big kitchen with a little pantry opening off from it. The kitchen was very basic with a fuel stove on one wall, a dresser that had shelves at the top for crockery, drawers for cutlery and a little cupboard for bread and two cupboards at the bottom where food was stored. On top of this was a set of canisters in which flour, sugar and tea was kept. In the middle of the room was a big pine table where Mum prepared the food and we ate our meals.

Through a door on the left of the kitchen was a long, very wide passage that led to the bathroom/laundry. In the weeks before Christmas Mum made lots of puddings and hung them along this passage on a strong rope. I remember touching them to see how hard they felt when I walked to the bathroom.

The bathroom/laundry housed the bath, a large round copper with a fire box beneath it to heat up the water and two big wooden wash troughs with a mangle in the middle of them. Water was heated in the copper, and then the clothes were boiled before being lifted with a stick into the first trough. Here they were rinsed, then put through the mangle to come out semi-dry into the second trough. The clothes were then taken outside and put on the line which was a piece of wire strung between two wooden posts. The posts were then angled so that the wire was low enough to reach then straightened once the line was full. This could be quite difficult particularly when big items like sheets and towels were hung on it. It's no wonder Australian housewives readily adopted the rotary Hill's Hoist when it became available during the 1950s.

The copper was also used to heat up water for our baths. Once the water was boiling it was siphoned into the bath with a piece of hose and then cold water was added. For years we three oldest girls bathed together and I remember later having baths with Jane and me at one end and John and Roger at the other. We always made them sit at the plug end.

Life before hot water services, washing machines and rotary clotheslines certainly wasn't easy.

When I was young we had an outside dunny but when sewerage eventually came to our street Dad built a small room on one side of the wide passage for the toilet. I was so pleased when this occurred, for it put an end to fearful night time trips outside to go to the toilet.

The bedrooms were all furnished with double beds and our girls' room also had a single bed. The boys slept together and so did Shirl and I. Jane was in a single bed until our youngest sister, Val, was old enough to share a double. Kids today don't seem to want to share a room with a sibling and would be horrified at having to share a bed, but I think it was quite a common practice in those days. I actually felt quite lonely in bed by myself when Shirl went to Melbourne to attend university there.

The parlour was generally only used on Sundays when Grandma and Pop visited and when we cooked crumpets at the fire in there. Nan sat in there to listen to the news on the wireless when she came to stay with us, but it certainly wasn't used much. During the war years she always wanted to hear the news and I was allowed to sit in there with her as long as I was quiet. I'd sit there, quiet as a mouse but not really understanding what was being said, but I just liked to be with her.

The hub of the house was of course the kitchen. The big pine table was where Mum prepared our food and also where we did our homework, played games and drew and coloured in when we were lucky enough to have pencils and paper. Mum cooked everything on the fuel stove and also cut all the wood to keep it going. It looked a very difficult thing to cook on but Mum loved it, and took quite a while to get used to an electric oven after we moved to Tower Road.

As I mentioned earlier Dad earned extra money by teaching at the Technical College two or three nights a week and umpired football during the season. During the summer he went fishing or rabbiting on the weekends, so he was often away from home.

When he was home he always seemed to have some project on the go. He built a dinghy in the back yard, bending the timber in a long metal thing that was heated up to make the wood pliable. He also made a net one winter. It was strung on a line that ran along the long room that went across the back of the house from the kitchen to the bathroom/laundry. You had to be careful when you went past not to get tangled in it.

Dad made some very interesting toys for us kids, for there were few ready-made toys available during the War Years. One year he made me an enormous wooden Donald Duck that walked when you sat on it and moved from side to side. It was a terrific idea but it proved to be very difficult to get it to move. It lasted a long time though and eventually rockers were put on the bottom of this toy and our own children played on it.

That same year Dad made Shirl a little wooden figurine that balanced between two posts and could be made to do somersaults by moving the sides.

Although Dad wasn't around all that much, and was busy when he was at home, he was a loving, affectionate man. He'd kiss us all goodbye before he left for work saying to Mum, 'Goodbye Duck,' then to each child in turn, 'Goodbye little duck.' He also always kissed Mum when he came home from work and any of us kids who were around. I grew up feeling loved and secure.

When we girls were older we wondered at how Dad had grown up to be such a loving man, for his mother, our Grandma, was a tough, undemonstrative woman. We were all a little in awe of her, and very quiet when she was around because she thought 'Children should be seen and not heard.'

The only thing Dad ever told us about his childhood was about his attempt at flying. I think it was shortly after he and his family moved to Lutana and he was eleven or twelve. There was a high quarry nearby and Dad thought his mother's big black umbrella would act like a parachute if he jumped from the top with it open. He sneaked the umbrella out of the house, then opened it up when he reached top of the quarry before leaping off. Evidently it turned inside out shortly after take-off and he went crashing to the ground. Surprisingly he didn't break any bones, for I have seen the quarry where he attempted this flight and it is very high. He was, however, battered and bruised and had difficulty walking. When he staggered home Grandma was more upset about the state of her umbrella than that of her son, and gave him a hiding. Hearing this story verified my opinion of her as a hard lady.

After Pop died Shirl, Jane or I sometimes stayed with Grandma in the rooms she lived in behind the shop that had belonged to Pop. My older siblings loved going there and even happily worked in the shop, but I only went once and hated it. I was worried all the time that I might do something to make her cross, was too shy to work in the shop and was frightened when she washed my hair because she rinsed it in nearly boiling water. It reminded me of being bathed by the square nurse in hospital.

Although she made milkshakes for me after school and sundaes every night for tea I wasn't happy staying with her. I remember spending ages doing elaborate drawings to decorate my homework so that I didn't have to work in the shop. I was glad when the visit came to an end.

Obviously she realised how unhappy I'd been because she told Mum I had missed my family too much. I was thankful that I was never expected to go again.

In contrast I adored our Nan, Mum's mother, totally. She was a tiny little lady with a very beautiful deep voice. When she visited she spent the time telling us stories or reciting long and exciting poems. She also listened interestedly to everything we had to say and treated us like young adults. During the last year she was alive I used to ride my bike to her place nearly every Saturday, and sit with her while she worked away crocheting colourful bedspreads. She was very artistic and made sure every coloured square harmonised with those around it. I remember us spending some time deciding whether or not pink could be placed next to a deep maroon, and feeling pleased when she agreed with my suggestion to put blue next to a particularly lovely shade of green. She fostered in me both a love of writing and art, and was an important influence in my life. My siblings and I are lucky enough to each have one of her paintings in our homes. She was a talented artist when young, but the burden of being widowed when her four children were in their teens seemed to have put an end to her painting.

On both sides of the family our grandfathers were dead, although Grandma had married a second time and we called her husband Pop.

Dad had an older sister who was our Auntie Pearl and a brother named Alf, who we didn't meet for many years. When we finally made his acquaintance he created quite a stir.

Mum had a brother, Don, who died very young from glass particles damaging his lungs. He had worked etching designs on glass without wearing a mask and this killed him.

She also had two sisters, Auntie Barb who we girls didn't like, and Auntie Ron who we adored. Both these Aunts drove cars, which was quite unusual in those days. Both had also lost their first husbands, but in very different circumstances.

Auntie Barb's husband drowned when they had only been married a short time. Evidently he dived off a yacht and drowned even though he was a good swimmer. We kids never knew any more than that, but when we were older and had grown to dislike Auntie Barb we used to say he'd probably done it to get away from her. She went on to marry a man called Bluey. I think she met him when she took scones to the soldiers who were stationed at Brighton Camp. He had red hair and laughing blue eyes and we kids liked him very much because he played silly games with us. He finished up in a mental institution of some kind because he had 'bad nerves'. Mum said he was shell shocked from being in the war, but we blamed Barb for him having a final nervous breakdown. She married for a third time but I only met that husband once. The only thing I remember about him was that he had a very damp, limp handshake. I think she finished up kicking him out of her house too.

Auntie Ron had two children with her first husband, but she divorced him because he had an affair with another woman. In those days you had to have grounds for divorce and the only ones were adultery, desertion or physical violence. The most common ground used was adultery, but you needed evidence this had been committed. According to Ron she did her hair in plaits, dressed up like a schoolgirl and followed her husband when he went to meet the other woman so that she could get the requisite evidence. I don't know whether or not this is completely true, for she was a very entertaining storyteller and she may have embellished the situation. After her divorce she had a period of freedom, and then married a man who adored her, but we thought very boring. Unfortunately after a short time he also bored her so it wasn't a deliriously happy marriage.

I always thought she might have loved that first husband most, and I think I got this impression from a little incident I've never forgotten. We were sitting in her car outside our house when she saw, in her rear-vision mirror, the 'naughty men' coming down the street.

These men were a usual sight, for they went up Windsor Street every Sunday morning and came down again at about lunchtime. I had heard Mum and Mrs Johns, our next-door neighbour, talking about them, and gathered that these 'naughty men' went up to the quarry to play a game called two-up. I understood from listening in on these adult conversations the game involved throwing two coins into the air and trying to guess whether they would come down heads or tails. This seemed to me a harmless enough game to be playing, but evidently they weren't meant to be doing it because they bet money on the outcomes and it was illegal to gamble.

On the day I was in the car with Auntie Ron she looked in the mirror and saw that her ex-husband was among the 'naughty men' and said, 'Keegan's there.'

She immediately whipped out her compact and dusted powder on her nose, then pulled her lipstick from her bag and drew on a bright red mouth.

I knew Keegan was her ex-husband, and couldn't understand why she would want to look nice for him, so I asked her why she'd put on the makeup.

She said airily, 'Oh Darling, one must always look one's best.'

As the men passed her car on the other side of the street Auntie Ron watched them. None of them looked our way.

When they'd gone I asked, 'Which one was him?'

She answered, 'The tall one in the brown hat.'

Thinking to cheer her up, for she looked sad I said, 'I didn't think he looked very nice.'

'Neither did I Darling,' she answered in a soft voice, but somehow I don't think she was telling the truth.

We didn't have many cousins, and Auntie Ron's two sons, Chris and Des, were the only ones we played with. Auntie Pearl's son Brian and daughter Joyce were much older than we were, and we didn't see Uncle Don's children after he died. Chris was about Shirl's age and we didn't like him much. Once he pushed me out of a dinghy when I was still only learning to swim properly. I went straight to the bottom and came up spluttering, then swam desperately for the shore. I still love swimming, but have always been rather fearful of swimming underwater and I blame Chris for this.

His younger brother Des was close in age to Jane and was nice. Jane and I had quite a few adventures with Des, which included eating unripe quinces that gave us awful stomach aches and being chased by a bull and jumping a six-foot fence to escape.

We also got into trouble once because of Des. He told us that you could use a pump to get warts on your skin. Now I can't imagine why we should want to get warts, but we thought we'd give it a go. Des suggested we pull our pants down and he'd try to pump warts onto our bottoms. We duly complied, and were seen by the lady who lived next door. She rushed over to our place and told Mum we were playing sex games in the garage. Mum came down, told us to pull up our pants and asked us what we thought we were doing. When we tried to explain about the warts she growled at us for being so silly, sent Jane and me to our room, and Auntie Ron took Des home. Mum then gave us a talk about not taking our pants off in front of any boy. Having time out in one's room is now considered the preferred way to punish a child who has been naughty. There's actually nothing new about this, for this was our mother's only form of punishment, and didn't happen often.

In our home a variation on this was being sent to the little dark box room at the end of the passage. I was the main child to have this punishment meted out to me on a fairly regular basis because I was a picky eater. In our house you were expected to finish off all your food, but I hated mince and curry. I liked most food, but I really couldn't stand either of these two dishes and refused to eat them. When I refused these dishes, despite being told there were children starving in China who would love my food, Dad would send me to the little room with the offending dish. Here I'd sit, watching the fat congeal around the mince or the curried sausages get cold until I was granted my freedom.

The room to which I was banished was only about two metres square and had a shelf running along one wall. This shelf held old books and newspapers. I had been sent to this room several times before I examined the contents of these shelves. Most of the stuff looked boring, but a big book with Medical Encyclopaedia on the cover caught my eye. I lifted it down and was leafing through it when I saw a strange picture. It was actually two pictures of the same man. In one he looked young and handsome, and in the other his dark hair was white and he had dark shadows under his eyes and deep lines running down the sides of his face. Underneath these pictures was some writing that said, 'This is the result of self-abuse.' I knew that the word abuse meant to hurt someone, and figured out self-abuse must mean to hurt oneself. I was quite baffled as to why the young man had chosen to hurt himself, particularly as it had had such a disastrous effect on him.

Later I told Jane about what I had seen in the book and she said she'd come with me and have a look at it next time I was banished, for we weren't allowed into that room except as a punishment.

The next time we had mince Jane also refused to eat, and the two of us were sent off with the offending dishes. As soon as we were in the room I showed her the book. We were pondering together just what 'self-abuse' could mean when Dad appeared at the door, 'I thought you two were up to something. What have you got there?'

He pulled the book from our hands and took it into the kitchen to show Mum. Jane and I huddled nervously in the room until he returned and said, 'Ok, you can come out, but if you don't eat your mince you're not getting anything else.'

Jane settled down and ate her mince, I went to bed hungry and the book disappeared forever from the little room.

It was years before we knew that 'self-abuse' meant masturbation, and that it didn't cause the diabolical effects described and shown in the big book. I've often wondered since what other misinformation was to be found in that rather imposing-looking Medical Encyclopaedia.

We grew up in a house virtually devoid of books. I think this was fairly common for during the war years there just weren't many children's books being produced. Besides the banned Medical Encyclopaedia, which certainly wasn't a children's book, I only remember two.

One that we spent many happy hours exploring was Cole's Funny Picture Book. It had a colourful cover with a sort of rainbow on it, but inside I think it was all black and white. The drawings I liked best were of funny faces that looked like another face when you turned the book upside down. Jane and I thought them very clever, and would sometimes try to draw faces like them.

The other book was an Arthur Mees Encyclopaedia. I believe they came in a set but I think we only had one of them, and the only thing I remember from it was a religious tale about Judgment Day. The illustration was in colour and the scene was a cemetery. There was a bright light in the sky, and people gathered around the graves while their loved-ones came up out of them. These people who'd been buried were all clean and so were their clothes. I'd played in enough dirt to know they couldn't possibly be so clean. Because of this the picture annoyed me, and I began to have doubts about some other things I was being told about God and Jesus. Mum had bought us up to believe God was in Heaven and watching over us. She said he had a big book and in it he wrote when any of us were good or bad. Quite a cunning way of ensuring all of her brood behaved themselves. After seeing that picture I began to have serious doubts as to whether what our mother had told us about God was true. That illustration in the book was obviously inaccurate so what could you believe?

Although we didn't have books to teach and entertain us Mum told us little made up stories and poems with moral messages, and our Nan was just wonderful. She was extremely well read and must have had a phenomenal memory because she could recite endless very long poems. My favourites were 'The Highwayman' and 'The Lady of Shallott.' She also told us all the Greek myths and legends as well as many stories about some of our ancestors and their early years in Tasmania. As I have mentioned earlier she had an enormous influence on me, even though she died when I was only ten.

Going to School

I remember being keen to go to school because I knew they had books there and I would learn how to read. Once Jane, the sister nearest in age to me, started school I couldn't wait to join her there. She was the one I'd mainly played with and I was lonely without her. My brother, John, was two years younger than I and Roger was a baby.

I started school when I was five and I remember being thrilled about getting dressed into my school blouse with a Peter Pan collar and my navy tunic with pleats in the front and the back. During the next ten years I was required to wear the same kind of shapeless navy tunic, and later at high school, thick navy stockings, a bowl-shaped hat and navy gloves were added to complete this totally unfashionable ensemble. In time I became heartily sick of this unattractive garment, but I loved my first tunic.

Getting ready for school was quite a business because Mum spent ages doing our hair. At that time the most popular child star in the world was a cute little girl called Shirley Temple. She was born in 1928 and I'm pretty sure our Shirley, who was born in 1934, was named after her although Mum insisted it was just because she liked the name. Anyhow the fashion at that time was for every little girl to have ringlets like the famous little film star. Shirl and Jane both had curly hair and Mum did their ringlets every morning, curling clumps of hair round her finger while we washed our hands and faces in a large dish of warm water. When it was my turn she would try valiantly to curl my straight thick hair around her finger, but the curls fell out. Sometimes she wound my hair around pieces of rag and I slept with it done in this way, although it was fairly uncomfortable. In the morning the rags were unwound and I had curls for a while, but they'd usually fallen out by the end of the day. Eventually Mum gave up trying to make me into a curly haired girl, and just brushed my hair then tied a ribbon to the front piece that always seemed to be falling across my face.

I grew up feeling that I was a bit plainer than my sisters because my hair was straight, for often Grandma and Aunty Pearl would look at me with critical eyes and say, 'It's a shame she didn't get the curls.'

Because of this early conditioning I was amused when I first heard of girls ironing their hair to get rid of their curls in order to have the much admired straight look that I'd had naturally.

While Mum did our hair she told us the story of Lonely Betty, a strange little tale about Betty, who had no friends at school until a rich and popular girl came to the school and befriended her. I think Mum made it up because it varied a bit with each telling, but for some reason we loved it. Another favourite was a long and very moralistic poem called 'Naughty, Naughty Nancy.' It was about a badly behaved child who ran away from home to the Land of Never Good, and of how her experiences there changed her.

Once we were ready Mum gave us each two pennies for our tram fare and watched us as we walked down Windsor Street to the Main Road. There we'd catch the tram to Derwent Park Road and walk to Moonah School. Two years after I started school Shirl went to high school so left earlier than the rest of us. This meant that by the time I was seven and Jane eight we became responsible for getting John, and later Roger, to school and home again.

When my granddaughter was about nine she brought home a message from her school informing parents that no child younger than ten should be allowed to walk to school unless accompanied by an adult. I know that roads are much busier and therefore more dangerous than when I was young, but are we now mollycoddling children too much? Have we taken away their sense of adventure that we free-range kids had?

I think perhaps we have.

Although Moonah School was threatened with closure a few years ago it has continued to function as a school. From the outside it appears to have changed little during the past seventy odd years, although there are now buildings in the part of the grounds where the girls played. The school was built in 1911, in red bricks, and consists of two main buildings. When I was young the front part was the infant school and I think may still be. The back part housed the primary school that was built around a quadrangle with rooms on three sides and the gymnasium on the fourth.

During my first year at school I was in the kindergarten room that was at the back of the infant school building and larger than the other classrooms. My teacher was Miss Walker, and she must have been a very tiny woman, for even to my five year-old eyes she seemed small. Sometimes when I got off the tram Miss Walker would be in front of me on the footpath, and I'd hurry to join the throng of children who always accompanied her down the street. We must have resembled a mother hen and her chicks as we hurried beside or behind her bustling little figure. I remember thinking she probably got her name because she walked so quickly.

We all loved her and I have fond memories of that first year at school. We had lots of paper and pencils to draw with and learnt songs and games. I particularly liked 'The

Farmer in the Dell' and 'I Had a Little Nut Tree'. Miss Walker also read lots of stories to us. It was quite a novelty to be read to because of the scarcity of children's books during the War Years.

One of my proudest times during that year occurred on Empire Day. This was an important day when I was a child, for most Australians still felt a strong tie with Britain. All the primary school classrooms had a large map on the wall and we were taught about the many countries that were part of the British Empire. I remember looking at those maps and being impressed by the number and spread of countries across the world that were coloured pink for this signified they were part of this vast empire. Australian children were encouraged to take pride in the fact that our country was part of it. Empire Day was celebrated in most schools with an assembly that ended with the singing of the National Anthem, God Save our Gracious King, and a salute to the flag. I think we may have also been given a half-day holiday, and many people celebrated in the evening by letting off fireworks around big bonfires.

When I was in kindergarten Miss Walker chose me to hold the flag because I had the straightest back. This meant that I stood next to my teacher and all the children in the infant school saluted. Boy did I brag about that when I got home.

My only unhappy memory of kindergarten was to do with the lunch basket. In those days there weren't fancy lunch boxes around, and everyone brought their lunch to school in a brown paper bag. When you were in the higher classes you kept your lunch in your desk. In kinder we didn't have desks, so all the lunches were put in a big cane basket. Mothers were meant to write their child's name on the bag, and I'm sure Mum always did, but one day I got the last one. It didn't have any name on it, and horror of horrors it contained jam sandwiches. Now I liked freshly made jam sandwiches, but never brought jam sandwiches to school because they went horrible and soggy after a while. I knew these weren't mine, and I looked around the circle of children to see who was eating my cheese and vegemite sandwiches, but I couldn't tell. I also knew Miss Walker wouldn't like me making a fuss so I unwillingly ate the wretched things.

From then on I made sure Mum wrote my name in very big print on my lunch bag.

The following year I had Miss Kippax, who was a sweet spinsterly lady. She was very religious and gentle and I had a happy year in her class. When I was in grade four Jane and I joined the Girls' Friendly Society and went to her little bible classes after school one day a week. We weren't particularly religious, but that year we were into joining or making up clubs so we added that to our list.

During her time at Moonah School Miss Kippax taught Shirl, John and me and met Jane through this society. She had a wonderful memory, as Shirl was to discover several years later in peculiar circumstances. I think Shirl was about eighteen, and she was waiting for a tram when a seedy-looking man approached her. He sat next to her in the tram shelter and started saying suggestive things. Shirl got up and was trying to get away from him when along came Miss Kippax. Seeing Shirl was upset she turned on the man, and in her best schoolmarm voice told him to go away and waved her brolly at him. After he'd scurried off she sat down and said, 'How lovely to see you Shirley. And how are Jeanette and Barbara and John getting on?'

Shirl was amazed that Miss Kippax recognised her after so many years, for the last time she had seen her Shirl had been a ten year-old child and now she was a young woman. She was also surprised that this dear old teacher remembered all of us and little things about us.

My next year was grade two, and I have forgotten it totally except for the first day. I don't even remember the teacher's name, but I have a memory of a slim woman in a navy dress with white spots and blonde hair pulled back into a tight bun.

On that first day we sat in our little desks and she called us out one by one to recite a poem. This had me worried, because although my Nan was always saying poems to us I didn't think I could remember one right through. The first six or seven children went out the front and said things like Humpty Dumpty and Baa, Baa Black Sheep. Now I knew these were rhymes, not poems, and thought the teacher would growl at them, but she just smiled and called the next name.

When she called my name I went to the front of the class as instructed, but said I didn't know any poems.

For some reason this made the teacher very angry. She said that of course I did and suggested I say one of the poems the other children had said. I didn't like to say they weren't poems for fear of hurting the other kids' feelings so I just stood there. This made her even angrier, and she picked up her cane and hit me around the legs. When I still refused to speak she caned me again then sent me back to my seat.

That's all I remember of grade two, which goes to show what a funny thing memory is, for I remember the trauma of being in hospital when I was so very young but have forgotten completely what must have been an unpleasant year when I was considerably older.

Moving from the infant school to the primary school was a big thing. It was almost like moving to another country. I'd heard about what it was like being in the 'big school' from my two older sisters and couldn't wait to get out of the rather cloistered part that was the infant school to the world beyond where there were exciting places in which to play. I think I also saw it as a way in which I would be sort of sharing this world with my sisters.

Grades three and four were mostly good for I had Mrs Avery both years.

There's always one teacher in a school who is everybody's favourite and she was the one. We girls all thought she was beautiful for she wore smart clothes, bright red lipstick and had an amazing collection of shoes. She always had spare pairs of shoes in her locker that was next to the blackboard in front of the class. After school she'd often change from the pair she had worn during the day to another equally interesting pair.

Like all teachers in the primary school she had a cane, but she never used it. Because she was so nice and made school fun no one was naughty in her classes.

One of the best times I ever had at school was in autumn in grade three. Mrs Avery decided we would have an autumn party, and we spent days bringing along apples and pears that were placed on the wide window ledges around the room. One of the kids supplied a big bag of walnuts and these were put with the fruit. Another day we were told to bring autumn leaves and several of us brought along small branches. I broke a branch off the next-door neighbour's quince tree and took that proudly to school. We also went on an autumn walk and picked briar berries that were growing at the side of the road and collected any fallen leaves we could find. When we returned to school the boys made collages with the leaves and we girls made necklaces and bracelets with the berries.

By the end of the week our classroom looked a picture and other teachers popped in to look at it, and kids from other classes cast envious eyes around the door.

On Friday we had weekly test as usual and reading, but we spent the afternoon singing, playing games and finally eating all the fruit and nuts. Mrs Avery even let us all out five minutes early. We thought she was wonderful to do this, but the poor woman was probably worn out from the festivities and glad to see the back of us.

There were a few of things that marred my otherwise happy years in grades three and four. One of these was that I was caned frequently, not by my beloved teacher, but by a man who taught the modern school kids. He was responsible for disciplining latecomers and I was frequently late during my grade three year.

That was the year Roger started school and Shirl was at high school, so Jane and I were responsible for getting the boys to school. By this time Mum had five of us to get ready and my youngest sister Val would have been a baby. I can imagine how difficult mornings must have been for my poor darling mother, but often we would make it to the bottom of the street in time to catch the tram only for Roger to discover that he didn't have something vital for him to attend school. Sometimes it would be his pencil, sometimes his piece of rag that we had for handkerchiefs and occasionally even his lunch. I was the fastest runner, so the other three waited at the tram stop while I raced up the hill to retrieve whatever item Roger needed to make his day complete. If I didn't run fast enough to get back before the tram came we all had to walk to school.

Because the boys were in the infant school they didn't get into trouble for being late, but Jane and I did. Once you were in primary school you had to be in the quadrangle by nine o'clock or the big slide doors were closed and those children outside were late. Often we would be running into the school grounds when the bell went. We'd rush John and Roger into the infant school then run like mad to the far side of our school building, only to see that big heavy slide close in our faces. All of the latecomers then stood in a frightened little knot for we knew what was coming.

After the morning assembly was over and the other children had marched into their classrooms the kids who were outside the slides were rounded up by this hated teacher. He then lined us up in front of his class and caned us all very fiercely around the legs. I know it hurt, and I remember comparing the stripes on our legs with Jane at recess time, but we sort of accepted it as part of school life. After a few mornings of this happening we heard that if you knew you were going to 'get the cuts' you should rub pine needles on the part to be caned and it wouldn't hurt as much. We tried this, but I can't say it made much difference.

Many years later I was a junior teacher at Glenorchy School and Mrs Avery was teaching there. We talked about how I'd been caned so often during the first year I was in her class, and she said that particular teacher's cruelty had made her very angry. She also told me how much his pupils had hated seeing the little kids lined up each morning to be caned. To show their dislike of him they gave him an elaborately wrapped Christmas present. It was a box containing a rope tied like a noose.

I heard later that he got into trouble for something he did to a pupil. I don't know whether it was for violent or sexual behaviour towards this child, but he was moved to a school in the north of the state. Shades of the way the Catholic Church dealt with paedophile priests in the past.

Besides the almost daily canings my other big problem in grade three was learning to write in ink. Until that year we all wrote our schoolwork in pencil, but now we could change to using a pen once our writing reached a certain standard. The pens were a piece of wood, about the size of a pencil with a pointed metal nib in the top. You wrote by dipping the nib in the inkwell that was in the middle of the desk. My writing was fairly bad so I was one of the last to make this change, and I found it very difficult. I seemed to manage to get ink all over my hands and smudges on my work. Mrs Avery was very patient with me, but often I was kept in after school to rewrite a messy piece of work.

Eventually I mastered the art of writing with a pen and ink, but it was always my weakest subject. I looked forward to going to high school for there you graduated to a fountain pen. This was a far superior implement for it had a sucking mechanism whereby you put it in a bottle of ink and drew ink into the cavity. Once filled the supply of ink lasted quite a long time before needing replenishment and a fountain pen didn't drip and smudge like an ordinary one.

There were many and various wonderful inventions created during the twentieth century, but to my mind one of the best was the biro.

During my grade four year a couple of very unpleasant things occurred.

For a few years nits had been a real problem throughout the school, and a nurse came regularly to check our heads. If you were found to have nits a message was sent home to your parents with instructions on what could be done to get rid of the nasty little critters. During that year all the kids in my family caught nits and it proved to be very difficult to get rid of them.

For some reason they weren't around when my children attended school, but there has been a resurgence of this problem in many schools during the past couple of decades. There are now shampoos and other treatments that appear to be effective, but back in the 1940s the only recommended treatment was to remove them with a special comb.

From the time Mum was informed that we had nits she spent every evening combing our hair with the nit comb over a piece of newspaper. When it was your turn you sat with your head bent over the paper while Mum carefully combed each strand of hair with a small metal comb. The nits looked just like tiny dots, but it was a pleasure to see them on the paper, for you knew if they were all combed out your head would stop itching. After each child's head had been thoroughly combed the piece of paper was burnt in the fuel oven.

When this treatment failed to get rid of these nasties Grandma intervened. She was firmly convinced that hot kerosene would kill them. We suffered hot kerosene-soaked towels being wound around our heads, and slept on pillows that smelt of the vile stuff. From this treatment we finished up with sore red scalps, but the nits persisted in Jane's and my hair.

Because the boys had short hair their nits were easier to get rid of, and Shirl was at high school, so wasn't being reinfected. Jane and I still had the problem though, so unwillingly Mum decided that we should have our hair cut shorter. As I have mentioned earlier Mum loved her girls having long ringlets, and even though my hair was straight she liked it long, but now she resigned herself to Jane and me having our hair trimmed.

There wasn't a hairdresser in the neighbourhood, but a barber had a business not far along the Main Road from Windsor Street. For many years the red and white barber's pole remained, but it has now been removed. There is a shop that sells old wares and collectibles on the spot where the barber used to be, and when I saw this I thought they should have kept that pole as a suitable reminder of a past era.

Mum gave us the money for the haircuts and sent us off with the words, 'Now tell him you just need a trim.'

At that stage in our lives we were both tomboys. We loved running free and climbing trees and high banks. As we walked along the street to the barber's shop we decided it would be nice to have really short hair that didn't get tangled in branches when we were climbing trees or take ages to dry after a swim.

When we arrived at the barber's he asked us how much we wanted off, and we told him we wanted our hair very short. There were no photos taken of us at this time so I'm not sure exactly how much he cut off, but I do remember feeling amazingly free and light-headed after having my heavy locks removed.

I also remember walking home feeling a bit concerned about whether Mum would be cross at the amount of hair we'd had shorn.

We walked in the door; Mum took one look at us and burst into tears. She didn't growl at us, but her tears were worse than any other punishment, for our mother didn't cry. We went to bed feeling sorry for what we had done, and decided we'd try to make our hair grow back as quickly as possible.

Having our hair cut did seem to get rid of the nits, for we had no more trouble with them. The school nurse was pleased, for she had recommended that all girls with long hair have it trimmed and many had.

There were two girls who had ringlets as nice as Jane's and Shirl's. These girls didn't wear school uniforms but pretty dresses in summer and pleated skirts and colourful jumpers in winter. Compared with most of us girls in our plain navy uniforms and white blouses they looked like little princesses. Despite their glamorous attire they too got nits, and the nurse must have sent a message home to their mother suggesting they have their hair cut. The next day we were all lined up in the quadrangle ready to march into school when a large, angry-looking woman opened the slide and stomped to the front of the assembled school. She then threw the offending letter down on the ground in front of the headmaster and said, 'My kids aint got nits and they're not having no haircuts.' She then stomped out.

We kids all stood there in shocked silence, and I remember feeling so glad I had a gentle mother who had done the right thing, even though it had upset her. I also remember feeling surprised by how fat and slovenly the woman looked because her daughters were always so beautifully dressed.

Those two girls never did have their curls cut off, but the nit problem eventually disappeared from the school.

The other really horrible thing that happened during my grade four year was that I was terrorised by two boys in my class. It began one day when I was walking home alone. These boys came up to me and said they wanted me to take down my pants. I was fairly naïve at this time, but because of the incident with Des and the warts, and also something else that had happened to Jane and me the previous year, I felt very threatened by what they were suggesting. I knew what they wanted me to do was very wrong.

These boys were Robert and Dennis; I remember their surnames but they will be old men now, or dead, so I won't reveal their identity, but they have my eternal worst wishes.

Robert was a big bullyboy with a very red face and Dennis was his small lackey. When I refused one of them grabbed hold of me while the other tried to remove my pants. Somehow I managed to get away from them and ran as fast as I could. I was shaking and frightened by the time I reached home, but I didn't tell Mum what had happened. Instead I told Jack about it.

This is where I must mention Jack, for he was such an important part of my childhood. He lived down the street from us, and he and his sister Pat were an integral part the group of children who we played with at home.

Jack had blonde hair and blue eyes and was tall for his age. We started school at the same time, but he finished up a year behind me because he repeated grade three. I don't think this was because he wasn't bright and I know he wasn't particularly naughty, but because he was one of the bigger boys he always seemed to get caught if lots of kids were misbehaving. As a consequence he spent quite a lot of time chopping wood for the classroom fires so missed out on some vital lessons.

Anyhow he was my best and most consistent friend through my growing up years, and I loved him. It was natural for me to tell him about my scare with Robert and Dennis. I think I probably hoped he'd deal with them, but he said he didn't think he could take on both of the boys. Instead he said he'd make sure he was always waiting for me near the slide when I came out of school, and he'd help me escape from them. This was the beginning of our long short-cuts home from school.

During the next few weeks or months, or however long it went on, Jack and I went home on a dozen different routes. If we saw Robert and Dennis going one way we'd go the opposite, and finish up in strange and unknown streets. We knew the general direction and were never really lost, but in this way we explored just about all of Derwent Park, Lutana and Glenorchy. Frequently we ended up at the Grove, which was the nearest thing we had to a beach in our area, and from there we'd backtrack home. We must have walked for miles on some of these long short-cuts, but for us they were adventures.

Sometimes Robert and Dennis would trick us and turn up unexpectedly. Fortunately we could outrun them. Although Jack and I quite enjoyed our jaunts into unknown places there was always the fear that those two nasty boys might get me.

Eventually I told Jane about what was happening, and she did something that was most surprising. Jane was a dreamy sort of kid who seemed to float through life. Unlike me she didn't like school much; didn't like the regimentation. Although she started school two years before me she finished up only a year ahead because she repeated grade four. Evidently she hadn't been able to learn anything from her first grade four teacher because she didn't like the way she looked. Jane was always losing things, and couldn't tell the time until long after I could. In some ways I felt older than she, and certainly more competent.

When I told her of my problem with the horrible boys I expected sympathy, not action. The next day she went up to Robert in the playground, said, 'Stop chasing my sister,' and punched him on the nose. He let out a yell and with blood streaming down his face went racing away crying.

From then on he stopped bothering me.

What with the canings for being late, the trials of learning to write with pen and ink, the nits and being terrorised by Robert and Dennis those two years I spent in Mrs Avery's class should have been totally traumatic, but I remember them as basically happy. It just shows how important a teacher can be in how a child views the world.

My most amazing teacher and undoubtedly my most unusual one was Mr Truscott.

I first met him when I was in the infant school and Shirl was still taking me to school. We joined the group of children who were escorting him down Derwent Park Road. Each day lots of kids waited for him to get off the tram, and vied for the chance to be one of those who held his arm while walking down the road. I was a bit in awe of him, for he seemed very tall and had a rather bony, gaunt face. Shirl said I must be very quiet so he wouldn't know I was there, because he didn't like little children chattering. Years later when I was in his class I told him about this, and he laughed and said he'd have loved to have met me then.

He had a name for being tough and caned both boys and girls if they misbehaved. Despite this most of us were very pleased when we were put in his class. Although he had an assistant he taught us arithmetic, listened to us read and was completely engrossing when he talked about the different countries in the world and the intricacies of the natural world.

He also gave us a wide knowledge of history, and I still remember the lesson in which he told us how people often got their names from the work they did, or as the son of someone. We had a Robertson and a Johnson in our class, as well as a Smith and a Ploughman. He explained that with names like Johnson and Robertson, boys were so named when their fathers were good and admirable men. Names like Smith and Ploughman related to the work these people did. He told us what blacksmiths and ploughmen did in those times and why their work was important. He finished the lesson with, 'And of course we all know about knights.' It made me very proud to be a Knight, for he'd told us earlier in the year about King Arthur and the Knights of the Round Table.

I have remembered this lesson for over seventy years because he made life in early England relevant to us through our names. He was truly a great teacher.

What made him even more amazing was that he was totally blind. His assistant wrote the spelling words and sums on the blackboard and took us through our times tables, but he did everything else.

Because he was blind he had extremely good hearing. He could pinpoint with uncanny accuracy which child was speaking when they shouldn't, and take unerring aim at the offender with a piece of chalk or the eraser.

Besides being a wonderfully stimulating teacher he did things with us out of school time. He had a three-seater bike he kept at school, and let his pupils ride it during lunch times and after school. He'd sit in the middle with a pupil front and back and ride around the school grounds. Once when I was riding on the front I unthinkingly went under a tree. I ducked and so did the girl in the back seat, but poor Mr Truscott was swiped across the forehead by a branch. He had quite a nasty gash and I felt terrible, but he said, 'These things happen.' Surprisingly he still let me ride the bike, but teased me about not taking him under any more trees.

He had a boat shed at Cornelian Bay and a few times took a mob of us there after school to swim off his jetty. We'd all walk there together, and then spend a happy time jumping off his little jetty and swimming in the then pure, unpolluted water. Afterwards we'd all escort him to a nearby bus stop before walking home.

Mr Truscott also had a shack. It was somewhere on the Eastern Shore, possibly at Dodges Ferry, but I'm not quite sure. Sometimes he took boys from the class there for the weekend. We girls thought this a bit unfair and asked him why we couldn't go, so he agreed to take a group of us if we could get permission from our parents. My two best friends and I were given the okay, although I know Grandma tried to talk Mum and Dad out of giving me permission. She thought it wasn't right for girls to go away with a male teacher.

In the end one of my friends got chicken pox and the other girl's parents changed their minds about letting her go. Of course I couldn't go by myself, but I was so upset Mum and Dad said I still could if Jane went as well.

We had a wonderful few days and Mr Truscott was a very easy-going host. He encouraged us to go off and enjoy ourselves, and we ran wild in these unfamiliar surroundings while he worked around his shack. Most days we came back early enough to cook the tea, but one day we got carried away playing a game pretending we were Robin Hood and Friar Tuck. We were so engrossed in our game we didn't return to the shack until it was nearly dark. When we apologised for coming back so late he laughed it off, then served up lamb chops with potatoes, carrots and peas, all beautifully cooked.

We must have told him about our game because when we were back at school, after the holidays, Mr Truscott said one day in class, 'I saw Robin Hood during the holidays.'

I blushed furiously, because I thought he was going to tell the whole class about Jane's and my game, and I would find this so embarrassing.

One of the cheekier boys said, 'But you can't see sir.'

He laughed and said, 'Well I must have imagined it.' Then turning his head in my direction he said, 'And imagination is a wonderful thing.'

You can see why we loved him.

On the last day at his shack his mother and grandmother had come down to take us home, bringing with them the most delicious Cornish pasties I have ever tasted. I was surprised that Mr Truscott still had a grandmother, for I had lost my beloved Nan the year before, and here was a grown up man with his still alive. I was also fascinated by the way this grandmother spoke, for she said English words, but in a funny way. When I told Mum about her she said it was because old Mrs Truscott was from Scotland, and that she had a Scottish accent. This was the first time it registered with me that people who lived in other countries spoke different languages.

One of the most daring excursions we went on with Mr Truscott was when he took a group of about fifteen of us up the mountain. We met in town, caught a bus to Fern Tree, and then walked to the summit. It was the first time I had been to the top of Mount Wellington and I was stunned by the view. We ate our sandwiches sheltering among rocks from a rather stiff breeze before walking all the way back along the track that came out at Lenah Valley.

It was a wonderful and memorable day, and I'm sure that at no time were any of us in danger. Nowadays there is no way one blind teacher would be allowed to take such a group anywhere without at least a couple of helpers, let alone up a mountain. I'm so glad I grew up in a time when the world was a freer and more trusting place.

As I have said earlier I was first caned in grade two and then caned for being late during my grade three year. By the time I was in Mr Truscott's class I was fairly immune to this form of punishment, and didn't find it unusual that this beloved teacher caned both boys and girls if they were naughty. Even though I was generally good I got the cuts from him a couple of times. Once it was for talking and I figured I probably deserved it.

The other time was when one of the boys changed the time on the clock in our classroom, putting the hands fifteen minutes ahead. The boy who did this was called Robert and was relatively new to the school. He came from another country, I think it might have been South Africa, and always wore khaki shorts and shirt and leather sandals of a sort none of us had seen before. He had blonde hair and green eyes and seemed to be tanned all the year. He had charisma and was admired by both the boys and girls, for there was something devil-may-care about him.

When he altered the time on the clock there were about eight of us in the room, and I remember giggling nervously at his bravado. His idea was that we would all be let out of school early, for it was Mr Truscott's responsibility to get a child to ring the bell that signaled the end of the school day. When it was getting close to three-thirty by the clock, the assistant told Mr Truscott the time, but he must have sensed it was earlier for he checked it on his brail watch. Somehow he worked out when the clock had been changed, for at three-thirty he let the class go except for the eight of us who had been in the room. He told us we'd be allowed to go when we gave the name of the person who'd altered the time on the clock. Dobbing was considered the worst possible thing you could do so we all sat there in silence, with Mr Truscott glowering in our direction with unseeing eyes. When it became obvious that no one was going to tell, he lined us up and we were all caned on both hands.

As we left the room he said, 'I'm disappointed in the lot of you.'

We all felt terrible, and from then my admiration of Robert waned. I also don't think he was ever as popular with the other kids again for we all thought he should have owned up once it became apparent we were all going to get the cuts.

During the year I was in Mr Truscott's class we celebrated Arbour Day by planting trees. I was chosen to do the honours, assisted by a boy called Kevin. I think we had done the best in the weekly test. The tree was an oak and I held it straight in the hole while the boy shovelled in the dirt, and then we both patted the earth down carefully. I watched over that tree all the time I was at Moonah School and throughout the years looked for it when I passed the school.

Some years ago, when I started writing this memoir I stopped at the school and went to look around. The slides have been removed and I could see into where the quadrangle used to be. The classrooms surrounding this square had been enlarged, leaving a small area filled with planters. It looked bright and cheerful and so much smaller.

The pine trees that grew along the fence line had gone, as had most of the girls' playing area, but my oak tree was still standing. It had had some branches lopped but still looked healthy. I couldn't resist taking a photo of it, and then had to explain why I was doing this to three women who'd been watching me. I told them I had helped plant the tree when I had been in Mr. Truscott's class.

I'm glad I went back for I learnt that there was to be a big centenary celebration at Moonah School. As part of the celebration a plaque was going to be put up in memory of Mr Truscott, who taught at the school for over thirty years, from 1938 to 1967. The women asked me if I would speak at the celebration and I agreed to. On the day I talked about what it had been like to be in his class. I mentioned riding with him on his three-seater bike around the school grounds, of swimming from his boat shed at Cornelian Bay and of our momentous walk up to the summit of Mount Wellington. I also said what an inspiring teacher he had been but that he caned us when we misbehaved. I have wondered since what the kids and teachers made of my talk about a teacher who loved his pupils and wanted to spend time with them out of school time but who also used corporal punishment when they stepped out of line.

He was certainly unique, as a teacher and a man and I'm glad his long years of service were recognised.

In my grade six year I had Mrs Hall, who had a name for being very strict but fair. I really enjoyed that year because she was a good teacher and I did very well in her class. I often got full marks in the weekly tests, and came top at the end of the year. My mother was very proud of me and said I'd followed in my father's footsteps. When she died forty-three years later we found the certificate I received that year among her treasures.

Despite my academic success I often got the cane. Sometimes it was for talking, but more often it was for eating in class. My best friend Yvonne and I sat in front of a nice but rather plump boy called Alan. He always seemed to have lollies and was very generous about sharing them with us. Unfortunately we were frequently caught so our names were put on the blackboard with a cross next to it. At the end of the day Mrs Hall lined up in front of the class all the children whose names were on the blackboard for being naughty and we were caned on both hands. She would get one very red cheek when she used the cane and look quite stressed. I was more worried that she would make herself ill than upset by the pain she inflicted.

During the second half of the grade six year we had lots of tests, for we were to sit the Ability Test at the end of the year, and this was to get us used to the kind of questions we would face. They tested your comprehension of written texts, word knowledge and mathematical ability as well as your general knowledge. I believe in some schools children didn't get this preparation, but at Moonah School we certainly did.

At that time there were only three high schools in Hobart. Hobart High was considered the most academic because languages were taught there as well as the more general subjects like English, Math and Science. It was also the only school from which you could matriculate. Technical High was an all boys' school where trade subjects were taught as well as the other more general subjects, and at Ogilvie High, which was mainly for girls, typing and shorthand was taught along with the general curriculum.

To get into one of these high schools you had to pass the Ability Test. If you failed this important test you went to a so-called Modern School. At that time the Modern Schools were just a few rooms in some of the primary schools that were set aside to house the 'failures'. Here these modern school students completed years seven to nine, filling in time until they were sixteen, or until they could get special permission to leave school and start work.

We had Moonah Modern School at our school and were quite in awe of these big kids, who didn't have to wear uniform so looked quite grown up. The girls wore full light, flowery dresses or tight straight skirts and sweaters and the boys wore long trousers and shirts or jumpers.

Although we were somewhat in awe of these big kids we didn't want to join them, for our parents had told us they would all finish up in dead-end jobs. Generally you needed to go to Tech to get into a trade, Ogilvie if you wanted an office job and Hobart High if you planned on entering a profession. The Modern School girls could only hope to work in shops or factories and the boys would mainly get jobs as manual labourers.

In retrospect it seems appalling that one's future could be determined by that one test taken by eleven and twelve year-olds, but we all accepted this at the time.

As the end of the year approached the frequency of the trial tests increased. I really enjoyed them, but I know all this testing made some kids very anxious. Yvonne became very nervous about it, and worried that she would fail. I spent a lot of time reassuring her she would be okay.

On the day of the test she looked almost green with nerves, and I was concerned about how she'd go. We all filed into the room and were given the first paper and so it began. I only remember writing furiously during each test, chattering nervously during breaks, and then back again to more furious writing. Finally it was over and we all filed out wearily.

I don't know how long it took before we got our results, but I remember clearly the day they came out.

Mrs Hall stood in front of the class with the list of successful students in her hand. When she called out our names we were to go to the front of the class, and I felt a sigh of relief when I heard my name called. I was thrilled when Yvonne's was called straight after mine.

We were all taken into the staff room and told which school we would be going to, and I was pleased that I'd got into Hobart High. Although it was still early afternoon Mrs Hall said we could all go home, for the children who had failed would be disappointed and wouldn't be able to share our excitement at having passed. She also said she knew that we'd want to tell our mothers as soon as possible.

By that time our family had moved from Glenorchy to New Town so I'd ridden my bike to school. I raced for the bike shed and rode home as fast as I could. Hot, sweaty and red-faced I rushed into the house yelling, 'Mum, Mum, I've passed.'

She just gave me a hug and said, 'Of course you have Darling. I knew you would.'

Mum always had such faith in our abilities, and told us all that we could do anything we set our minds to. She was also the one with whom we wanted most to share our little triumphs in life. When I received my first term reports, while doing matriculation as a mature-age student of thirty-six, Mum was the one I showed them to first, not my husband or my teenage children.

School Days in the 40s

So far I have only given snippets of what school life was like back in the 40s, the journeys to school, the various teachers I encountered, the canings and nits. Schools are so different now, and the school days appear to be less structured than they were in the 40s. In the mornings children now wander into their classrooms and key into computers, put their home reader back on a shelf and choose the next one that takes their fancy or stand around talking to their friends until it is time for class to begin.

Our school days were much more regimented. We all assembled in the quadrangle in our classes, unless you were late and locked out. After morning assembly Mrs Avery played some stirring tune on the piano and we all marched into school. The days always began with spelling, dictation, mental and arithmetic. We spelt our words in unison, wrote our dictation then chanted together the multiplication table we were learning. Next we did the sums that were written on the blackboard and had them marked. This only varied when we had a new mathematical process to learn.

By then it would be recess time and after a brief race around the playground we returned to our classrooms for reading and composition. These subjects took us up to lunchtime when we were free for an hour.

The afternoons were less structured and more varied. We had geography, nature study or history, as well as some fun subjects like art, music and physical education. We had quite a large gymnasium, but I don't remember what equipment we had in there except for the three heavy ropes that hung from the ceiling near the stage. I mainly remember these because in grade five I was the only girl who could climb the ropes right to the ceiling. My years of picking up younger siblings and climbing trees had evidently paid off in helping me develop strong arms.

Every Friday we had the weekly test. We were tested on a piece of dictation and some spelling words, some quick mental arithmetic and then had to do ten sums. We were given marks out of ten for each subject, and if you got 30 or 29 your name was called out in assembly and you got to stand out the front. I loved these tests and managed to do pretty well in them.

It is now considered politically incorrect to have children pitting themselves against each other in this way. The new educational theory is that this sort of thing is unfair to the children who can't hope to achieve top results. They now aim for a personal best instead. Quite frankly I consider this way of thinking complete rubbish, for the world is a competitive place and I think these tests prepared us for the competition we would face in later life. They also gave the bright and average kids something to aim for.

This idea of children achieving their personal best is a term that has been borrowed from the sporting arena. We see elite sportspeople happy to achieve their personal best, but they sure are a whole lot happier with a gold or silver medal.

Well, enough of that. I'll get off my soapbox and return to describing my school.

The classrooms were fairly drear compared with those of today. There were tall windows along one wall that let in quite a lot of light, but the windows on the other side faced the quadrangle so were fairly dim. A slightly raised platform ran across the front of each room and on that wall were the blackboard and a map of the world showing all those pink countries that were part of the British Empire.

The ceilings were high and, as the only source of warmth came from a fireplace in the front of the classroom, we were generally cold in winter. Many of us wore a little bag impregnated with eucalyptus or Vick's Vapour Rub around our neck. This was supposedly a protection against getting colds or the flu. It may have worked because, except for when I had whooping cough, I don't remember having a cold during my years at primary school.

I do remember vividly having itchy fingers and toes from chilblains. A lot of children suffered from this complaint back then although it seemed to have ceased to be a problem by the time my children were attending school. All children walked at least part of the way to school for few people had cars and there were no school buses serving our area. I think the winters were colder then too because the mountain was covered in snow for many months and there was ice on the puddles most mornings during the winter. Of course we jumped into these puddles or broke up the ice with our fingers. As a result we were cold and sometimes wet by the time we arrived at school. We then had to sit in these sparsely heated rooms, the smells of wet socks and eucalyptus permeating the chilly air. When recess time came we ran around to get warm or huddled close to the fire if it was too wet to go outside.

I think the only people who were warm in those classrooms were the teachers who had their desks next to the fireplaces. It was rumoured that one of the teachers used to stand near the fire and lift her skirt to warm her bottom, but I don't know whether or not this was true as I was never in her class.

Our desks were all designed for two pupils. Each desk had a wooden seat that we sat on and a sloping wooden top that opened up. In here we kept our exercise books, our reading book and our lunch. There was a piece of wood on which the top hinged and in the middle of this piece was the ink well. Once we started writing in ink this was filled up by the ink monitor every day.

There were no class libraries in those days and our only reading matter was our reading book, which I loved. Each year you had a new reading book, but I only remember bits and pieces from them. One book had an excerpt from Silas Marner, where he finds the little girl sleeping and thinks her golden curls are gold coins. Another had a quite exciting little piece about Red Indians, and I didn't realise until I read 'The Last of the Mohicans' at university that the excerpt was taken from that. We were being surreptitiously introduced to the classics.

When I was at Teachers' College in the 1950s we were shown old copies of these readers and the language surprised me. Many of the words were almost archaic and the general vocabulary was far more advanced than that which was being taught only a few short years later.

Most of the classrooms were painted in fairly dreary colours, but to brighten them up there was a print of a famous painting in each room. Two that I remember are 'The Laughing Cavalier' and 'The Blue Boy'. I guess these were another small attempt to introduce a little bit of culture into our lives.

During lunchtime we played games, many of which are still played today; hopscotch was a favourite, as was 'What's the Time Mr Wolf'. A variation on that game was where one child facing a wall called out different letters and if you had that letter in your name you advanced one step. I liked this game because my middle name is Elizabeth and often the girl calling the letters would say Z thinking no-one would have this letter in their name and I would catch her unawares. We also did a lot of skipping, mainly with a long rope, and we'd see how many girls could get in at the same time.

I loved playing marbles and I had a bag of them, but generally the boys at school wouldn't let girls play. I had to be satisfied with playing against Jack and my younger brothers at home.

Most of the time girls played on the asphalt area to the left of the school or in the rather neglected area beyond. Here there were high weeds that we twined together to make cubby houses. Often we made necklaces and bracelets with the wild daisies that grew in abundance. There was also a weed we called soldiers that had a rounded top on the end of the stalk, and with these we played a gentle war game wherein you hit one another's soldier until one of the heads fell off. The other game we played with the weeds was a rhyme game for which you needed a particular plant that had alternate spikes growing out of a central stem. As you pulled off these pieces you chanted 'Tinker, tailor, soldier, sailor, rich man, poor man, beggarman, thief, doctor, lawyer, Indian chief. Whichever word you said when you pulled off the last piece described who you would marry. I remember being inordinately pleased when a rich man was to be my destiny and upset if the plant determined I would marry a beggarman or thief. For some reason we found this game immense fun and half believed the results, even though the next time you played produced an entirely different result.

The boys played on the front oval and on the asphalt area between the infant and primary schools. For a long time the front oval was a maze of tunnels and a marvellously exciting place to play, but girls weren't allowed there. These tunnels had been dug to house the children if enemy aircraft attacked Hobart during the war. I was in the infant school until nearly the end of it so didn't get to go into them, but Shirl and Jane said they'd had practice runs when they'd all had to don gas masks and run with their class groups to these shelters. They also told me they had to hold a rubber between their teeth, but I had no idea how this was supposed to help in the event of an air raid. It was only while writing this that it occurred to me it may have been a cunning way of keeping a bunch of noisy, excited children quiet for it would have been virtually impossible for them to speak with rubbers clenched between their teeth.

Eventually the tunnels were filled in and the oval once more became a sports ground, but it was still the boys' domain. There they played football and cricket, as well as running and chasing games. We girls rather envied the boys' extensive playing area, but perhaps our weed-filled patch was more exciting.

Every year we had a school fair. I think they mainly took place in the quadrangle for I seem to remember stalls set up around the edge of it.

The highlight of the fair was the pedlars' parade, in which all the children who had dressed up and been pedlars walked around in a circle and the best costume was judged.

I went in this one year but don't remember what I wore. I do know Mum made me toffee apples to sell, and Dad made a little tray with a ribbon that went round my neck. I also remember being glad when my last toffee apple sold, and I could hand over the money I'd made and get rid of the tray. It hadn't been much fun, trudging around trying to get people to buy from me while the other kids played. I didn't ever do that again.

The most memorable fair for me was the year of the balloons. Once again Mr Truscott was involved in this because he obtained the big cylinder of helium gas. The day before the fair he supervised the filling of dozens of balloons and we girls in his class tied several of these together. These floating balloons were put in the gym, obviously tied down to something so they didn't float to the ceiling, which was very high.

I know helium-filled balloons are old hat now, but this was the first time any of us kids had seen them. Our class was responsible for selling them, and they were very popular. The only problem was these balloons were such a novelty many children didn't hold on to them tightly enough, and soon lots of them were to be seen floating away in the clear blue sky. I thought they looked rather wonderful, but I don't imagine the kids who'd lost their balloons shared my feelings.

The school ball was another annual event, and was held in a hall in New Town.

Only primary school children went to the ball, and according to my older sisters I made a show of myself the first time I went.

Shirl was in grade six and Jane in grade four when I was still in the infant school. I must have made a fuss about not being able to go because Mum took me, on the understanding that I'd be a good girl and sit with her all evening. For most of the evening I was good, and sat with Mum and the other mothers watching the big kids twirl around the floor. They seemed to be having such a lot of fun and I wanted to join in, but knew I wasn't allowed.

When Mum was talking to another lady I wandered off towards the back of the hall and went through a door. I found some steps so went up them, and discovered that they led to the stage where the band was. I watched from the side for a while, but then felt an overwhelming urge to dance. Off I went prancing around the stage and waving my arms about in what I imagined was the way a ballerina danced. My time in the spotlight was short-lived because only too soon Mum came and removed me, and told me I'd been a naughty girl. I knew she wasn't really cross with me because she was laughing.

My sisters were very angry though, because everyone knew I was their sister and I had, 'made a show of myself.' It took me quite a while to live that down.

When I could go to the balls legitimately I enjoyed them, and Mum always made us pretty dresses to wear. I had a photo in one of these ball gowns, and I think I was about ten when it was taken. Although the photo was in black and white I remember that the dress was pink satin and there were sequins decorating the neckline. In this photo I have soft ringlets and a ribbon around my head and tied in a bow. Obviously, despite the odds, Mum was still persisting in trying to make me over in the image of Shirley Temple.

During the months leading up to the balls we had dancing lessons. These took place in the gym after school, and everyone planning on attending the ball was expected to go to them.

Mrs Avery played the piano and taught us several different dances. We learnt the barn dance and the military two step as well as how to waltz and do a quick step. She also told the boys what to say when asking a girl to dance and how we should respond.

These dancing classes were fun, and quite a few little boy\girl friendships began during them.

The social event that I remember most fondly was our grade five social. I think it was Mr Truscott's way of teaching us how to behave in a social situation, for it was discussed in class long before it took place. It was to be held in the gym and would be just our class. We were going to have games and dancing, and then go to supper. Before the night he told the boys that they must ask a girl to accompany them to supper, and that we girls must accept or reject their offers politely.

Mum made my dress from scraps of material she either had already or scrounged from Auntie Ron, but it was quite beautiful. It was aqua blue with a full skirt that came just below my knees and had puff sleeves. At the neck she inset a yoke made of a piece of material patterned in pink, cerise and black and she made a sash out of the same material. With it I wore new patent leather shoes.

Perhaps my description doesn't do the dress justice, but I can assure you it was lovely. I had a wonderful time at the social and had four boys ask to escort me to supper, more than any other girl in the class. I went to supper with a cute dark-haired boy who was a good footballer. I hope I rejected the other three politely.

Walking Home from School

Until John was deemed old enough to go home from school alone Jane and I looked after him. We either caught the tram home or walked along the road, and used the penny saved in tram fare to buy an ice block at a shop on the way.

After John turned seven he was on his own, and also responsible for getting Roger home. This wasn't anything thought out in great detail at the time, but looking back this is what happened.

Often Jane and I still walked home together, but now we didn't have to worry about the boys we went on different routes.

Sometimes we walked along the railway line as far as Derwent Park Station and then returned to the road. Other times we followed the line all the way out to Glenorchy Station and then had to backtrack. You really weren't supposed to walk along the railway line because a train could come along and run over you, but we knew there weren't many trains so did it anyway.

When we were feeling particularly daring we took an exciting little detour when walking along the railway track and went into a round concrete culvert. This ran along the side of the track, and was big enough for us to walk in if we crouched down. Water ran through at our feet and there was slimy green stuff along the sides. Once we had gone a bit of the way it was pitch black and scary. It seemed to take forever before we could see the small circle of light that indicated we were nearly through.

Doing this scared us, but every so often we walked the tunnel just for the hell of it. Obviously children get some twisted pleasure out of being scared. The brothers Grimm must have recognised this for they wrote scary tales that remained popular for decades. Now we have Harry Potter, a series that started out being relatively benign, but became increasingly scary as time progressed. And the kids love it.

During the time I was being harassed by Robert and Dennis, Jack and I discovered many different routes to home. With all these long short-cuts we must have been getting home pretty late, but our mothers didn't seem to worry about us. Mum was happy as long as we were home in time for dinner.

In our household dinner, or tea as we called it then, was at five o'clock. Our Dad worked at the Zinc Works, and zinc workers expected their tea on the table as soon as they arrived home. They started work at a quarter to eight and had lunch at twelve so were probably very hungry by five.

Anyhow we knew the rule and made sure we were home in time except for one day when Jane was late. I'd come home with Jack so didn't know where she was.

Mum dished out everyone's dinner and put Jane's aside. We all sat down to eat, but I could see that Mum was getting worried. During the meal she asked me when I'd last seen my sister, and I said I hadn't seen her after school.

After the meal Mum went outside and looked down the road. She came in and I heard her and Dad talking in their bedroom. They sounded worried. Dad was getting changed to go to the Technical Night School where he taught maths and technical drawing two or three nights a week.

By six o'clock they were both really worried and Dad said, 'I'm going to take the car and see if I can find her anywhere. Are you sure you don't know where she was going after school Babs?'

I had no idea where she was and told him so. I began to feel terribly worried because obviously Mum and Dad were upset.

When Dad went outside to get in his car he saw Jane at the bottom of our street. He stood there glowering as she walked slowly up the hill. She arrived looking a mess. Her hair ribbon was coming undone and she had dirt on her face and hands. In those dirty hands she held a bottle containing muddy-looking water.

Dad glared at her and shouted, 'Where the Hell have you been until this hour?'

Jane looked up at him smiling and said cheerfully, 'Tadpoling.'

Dad said, 'Get that smile off your face. And get inside.'

Jane got a belting, a very rare occurrence in our home, and was sent to bed without any tea.

I think from then we made sure to be home before tea, but it didn't stop our free ranging.

Our Street

We played outside most of the time after school and at weekends, for we lived in a wonderland of places in which to have adventures. At that time our street was surrounded by open spaces and we made them all our own.

On our side of the street there was a veritable mansion surrounded by extensive gardens. We didn't actually get to play much in those gardens for this property belonged to an old couple, and we were only allowed in there when their grandchildren lived with them for a year. Their father was fighting in the war and that was the reason they moved in with their grandparents for that time. They were rather fragile-looking kids with fair skin and freckles. Because they didn't like playing imaginary games and weren't allowed to climb trees we didn't think them much fun, but we loved wandering in the gardens so we put up with them.

This property filled up nearly half of our side of the street. Next to it was an empty block, then our house and about four houses above us. On our side of the road the blocks were all very big and backed onto a paddock where cattle sometimes grazed. Beyond this paddock was the football ground.

At the bottom of the other side of the street was the grocer's shop then nearly all weatherboard houses all the way up to the top paddock. Running across this paddock was a track that led to a large solitary house. Most of the houses were ordinary looking three bedroom houses similar to ours, but the one diagonally opposite us was a big bungalow-style house with a tiled roof and a lot of land at the side with a tennis court. The rest of the houses on that side of the road were on relatively small blocks and they backed onto a paddock that had a quarry in the middle of it. On the far side of this paddock was the avenue and next to that was Lenton, the house where Mum had lived for the first twenty-five years of her life.

Even in retrospect it appears to me Windsor Street was a world apart; not really belonging in the more northerly suburb of Glenorchy but also not a part of Derwent Park that was the suburb on the other side and where we went to school. I think this seeming isolation fostered a sense of community in the street and especially amongst the kids living there.

The grocer at the bottom of the street was a rather cheery fellow and we quite enjoyed dropping Mum's weekly order in to him and having a chat. The shop seemed to be varying shades of brown. There was a long brown counter where he stood and behind him were brown shelves containing tins and packets of different things. On the floor were hessian sacks of brown potatoes and brown onions and he had a large windows that came down nearly to the floor which had a brown painted trim all around it. The only clearly differently coloured item I remember were his scales, which were silver. He used these to weigh out the sugar and flour, which he then put in brown paper bags. It was all a far cry from the supermarkets of today.

Next to his shop lived people we didn't like very much. The man was little, aggressive and said to be a drinker. His wife had very short hair and a straight thin body so we thought she looked like a man. They had one daughter who was a bit older than Shirl. I only remember talking to her once for any length of time, and that was when she told us her version of the facts of life. According to her when a man liked a woman he took her out to dine, and then she would start expecting a baby. None of it made sense to me so I didn't believe her. I asked Mum what going out to dine meant and she said going out for a meal in a nice place. I was still confused so told Mum what the girl had said. She said it was a lot of nonsense and not to take any notice of her.

Next door to them lived the Smith boys, John and Brian. Although we played with them a lot I don't think we went to their house because I don't remember their parents. There was a house between theirs and Jack's place, where a young family lived with their baby. We spent a bit of time at Jack's house, but his mother had bad nerves so we usually played outside. We liked her and she was always nice, but even to us kids she seemed a bit fragile. I think this feeling about her was reinforced by the fact that the father did an awful lot of the things around the house that we only ever saw our mother do. Jack's father often bathed them and cooked their tea and I even remember him making faces on milk arrowroot biscuits with chocolate icing, currants and glace cherries for a birthday party. I certainly couldn't imagine our Dad ever doing that.

The next house up the street was the big one with the tennis court. It belonged to people whose sons were grown up men. We thought they were very rich because they owned big trucks and Mum said they had quarries. The father and older brothers were big solid men, and very scary. The younger brother was not as big and quite handsome. When he married he built a brick house on the land next door to our house, but he didn't seem to mind us playing in the pine trees at the bottom of his block so we liked him.

Another Smith family lived opposite us, although they weren't related to John and Brian. They were a nice friendly couple, but a terrible thing happened to them and from then they always seemed sad. Their only daughter died when the plane she was travelling in crashed. She had been for a holiday in Melbourne and evidently the plane's engine failed as they were coming in to land. They crashed into the sea somewhere off Seven Mile Beach and everyone on board was killed. She was the first person I had known who had flown, so I gained the impression air travel was very dangerous. When I was seventeen I flew from Launceston to Hobart at the end of my college year and was nervous all the way. We hit turbulent weather while crossing the mountainous region in the centre of our island, and I was firmly convinced we would crash despite the air hostess's reassurances.

I stayed with these neighbours when Mum was in hospital having our youngest brother. I think Mrs Smith liked having a little girl to look after again for she was very nice to me, but the thing I remember most about my stay there was that I got a splinter in my bottom. This happened when Jack and I were playing on the long wooden swing at the Grove during one of our extended wanderings home from school. It didn't hurt much until I got into bed and then it began to ache like crazy. Every time I moved it throbbed, and I imagined it was going deeper and deeper into my flesh.

Mrs and Mr Smith had friends in for a card evening, and I was too embarrassed to tell her about the splinter for I would have to show her my bottom. After the incident with Des and the pump I knew it was wrong to go around exposing this part of my anatomy. Finally Mrs Smith came in to check if I was asleep and I blushingly told her what was keeping me awake. She removed the offending splinter with a minimum of fuss and I was most grateful to her.

During that time Shirley and Jane had been allowed to stay at home with Dad but at ten I wasn't considered old enough. I did get to spend the weekend with them though and on the Saturday Dad went out, to umpire a football match I think. We hadn't seen Mum for a week so thought we'd visit her. In those days unaccompanied children were not allowed into the hospital so Shirley, who was fourteen dressed up in one of Mum's suits and a pair of her high-heeled shoes. I thought she looked very grown up and so did Jane and we were sure we would be able to fool the hospital staff. We caught the tram into town and walked to the hospital. Shirley teetered across in unfamiliar high heels to the admissions desk and asked, in her most adult voice, where Mary Knight's room was. The person behind the desk said children couldn't visit the wards without an adult so Shirl knew her cover had been blown. I couldn't understand how the woman had known for I thought Shirl looked very grown-up but I think she was just embarrassed. She hurried us back through the hospital entrance doors with us all feeling disappointed and dejected. We were walking unhappily down the driveway when we heard our mother's voice and she was standing high up on a balcony and waving to us. She looked so lovely with her black hair held back with a blue ribbon and a big smile on her face. Despite not being able to visit her we went home happy just because we'd seen her. I have wondered since if some kind soul ran up the stairs to tell her about her daughters trying to get in to see her so she could be on the balcony to wave to us.

Auntie Ella lived next door to the Smiths with her husband Roy and an ancient smelly dog called Laddie. After both husband and dog died we girls sometimes spent the evening and night with her to keep her company. None of us liked this as there was only one bed so you shared it with Auntie Ella. She was a fat soft woman and she wore her underclothes to bed. These consisted of a big boned corset and an enormous bra, both in a particularly strange shade of pink. She smelt of talcum powder and old woman, and I slept so far to my side of the high hard bed that one night I fell out. I don't think I stayed there after that, so perhaps the poor dear realised I found her an unpleasant sleeping partner.

Two doors up from Auntie Ella lived a rather glamorous lady who I think had lost her husband in the war. She had a border called Sid. He was a dapper little man who worked at the Zinc Works and always carried a Gladstone bag. Sometimes Jane and I would see him getting off the train at Derwent Park and walk home with him. We liked Sid but felt sorry for him. His landlady always seemed to be going out with different men. We could see her from our front garden as she came out of her house dressed up in a pretty dress and high heeled shoes. We'd watch as a man friend escorted her down her path and into his car, and think poor Sid must be lonely with her going out all the time. Mum said he wouldn't mind because he was just the boarder, but we thought we knew different. We were sure he was in love with her, and would have wanted to be the one taking her out.

A friend of our Nan's lived in the last house before the paddock. She was a nice elderly lady, and she had a beautiful garden that was full of flowers. Nan took me to visit her once but I picked some of the flowers while they were having afternoon tea and this upset my little Nan. I don't think her friend minded but I wasn't ever invited back.

The lady who lived next door to us and who had told Mum we were playing sex games with Des in the garage was a little whiny woman with very thin hair and faded watery eyes. She spent ages talking over the fence to Mum and always seemed to be moaning about something. She had a little strutting husband who we didn't like because we once watched him cut the tails off some tiny puppies and thought him very cruel. I think he might also have bashed up his wife on occasion, or at least that seemed to be what she told our mother.

They had several grownup children and their youngest was a couple of years older than Shirl. One of them was named Marge, and she helped Mum with us kids as well as some of the household chores. She kept an eye on the rest of us while Mum was busy feeding or bathing the current baby or took said baby for a walk in the pram. She also helped with the washing and ironing. I think Mum paid her a few shillings for this, but basically Marge helped because she was fond of our mother and us kids. We all loved little Marge for she was a cheerful presence around the house and I know Mum was grateful for her help. Actually she and one of her sisters attended all our weddings so obviously Mum kept in touch with them after we moved.

Barbara Knight

My First Trip to Town.

With the exception of the long journeys down to our shack at Connellys Marsh, Windsor Street and the surrounding open land plus the road to school was virtually all I knew of the world until we moved to New Town. My childhood years were rather like those of many English people during the early part of the nineteenth century who never ventured further than the outskirts of their village. Because of this relative isolation the memory of my first trip to the city has remained indelibly imprinted on my memory. It took place when I was about six so I think I must have been recovering from my bout of whooping cough. There was a photo, since lost, taken of me in a city street in which I look skinnier than usual. I am wearing a pleated skirt with a matching jumper, there is a gap where my two front teeth are missing and I have fat, false-looking curls. Altogether not a flattering vision so it's probably good that the photo is gone.

Mum used to go to town once a month to pay the accounts she had at two of the main shops in Hobart, Brownells and FitzGeralds. She must have taken me this time because I was home sick, and she probably thought it would be a treat for me. It certainly was. I had never been on such a long tram trip and remember sitting with my face glued to the window as we sped past the shops in Moonah then through the more residential area of New Town until we came to North Hobart and once more shops lined much of the street. I'd had no idea there was a world like this that was so different from the one in which I lived. When we finally reached town I was amazed because this was all shops, there were people everywhere and more trucks and cars than I had ever imagined existed.

Mum held my hand tightly as we got off the tram and walked up a street and then into a big, brightly lit shop. I had only ever been into the small suburban shops of our grocer and butcher and to me this huge department store looked like a sort of fairyland. There were lots of counters and at each one people were selling different things. Mum bought me a pair of woollen gloves and also told the lady behind the counter she wanted to pay money off her account. She handed the lady some money as well as a piece of paper that must have been the account. These were put into a little metal cylinder that was attached to wires that ran from the counter to up high near the ceiling where I could see a man sitting in a little glass room. I watched fascinated as the little cylinder zoomed up the wire and into that room. I saw the man take out the money and account, do some writing and then put something back into the little cylinder. This then came zooming back down and the lady at the counter gave Mum a piece of paper and some change.

This was the highlight of my trip to town for I had found the whole procedure totally fascinating and a bit mystifying. We went into another wondrously big shop where Mum paid her monthly account and then she said she'd take me to a café for a treat as I'd been such a good girl. In the café Mum ordered a glass of milk for me and tea for herself and scones for us both. We then sat down at one of the little round tables and a girl in a pinny brought us our drinks and the scones with little bowls of jam and cream. This was the first meal I had ever had away from home or at a relative's place and I remember feeling quite grown-up as I took a scone and put jam and cream on it for myself.

After we finished our treat we caught the tram home and the excitement of the day must have tired me out because

I fell asleep almost as soon as the tram started and Mum had to wake me up when we arrived at our stop.

As we walked hand in hand up our street she said, 'Your big day in town must have tired you out Sweetheart. Perhaps you still weren't well enough.'

All I could say was, 'I loved it Mummy.' I sighed with contentment and hoped Shirl and Jane would be home from school so I could tell them all about the big shop with the wires running up to the man in the glass box.

I think this was the only time I ventured outside of my suburban surrounds until I was a teenager so in a way our lives were very insular

Free-Ranging Weekends

Although the world I lived in may have been limited I never felt that it was because we kids were free to wander in our small domain. The houses opposite us had quite small back yards but on our side of the road they were enormous. Our own back yard had quite a slope and ended in a paddock. The yard was partially divided by a high, slightly falling down fence and a row of light green trees. You could sit on top of the fence and be amongst the trees.

Between the house and this fence was an area of rough grass. This was where Dad built his dinghy and where the clothes were hung out to dry on a long line. To one side of this was the garage, and on the other side was a structure that housed the outside toilet and the woodshed. Honeysuckle and a highly perfumed pink cabbage rose grew over this and onto the roof. This was one of my favourite possies on a summer day for it was warm and the smell was quite wonderful.

The last time I sat up there was a few weeks after my Nan's death. She had died two days before my tenth birthday and sixteen days before my youngest brother was born. The excitement of turning ten, having a new baby brother and the approaching summer holidays had filled my life, and stopped me dwelling too much on my little Nan's death. As I was sitting up there, enjoying the smells and the warmth radiating off the tin roof, I suddenly heard my Nan's voice saying clearly in my head,

"Break, break, break

At the foot of thy crag oh sea,

And I would that my tongue could utter

The thoughts that arise in me."

This had been one of my favourites, so I tried to think of the rest. I was going well until I came to the line,

"But O for the touch of a vanished hand

And the sound of a voice that is still."

Suddenly I was hit with the realisation that I would never see or hear my Nan again and I burst into tears. I cried and cried, until the roof cooled around me and I heard my mother calling my name anxiously from the back door.

After that I couldn't ever bring myself to go up there again.

Under this possie was the toilet which I disliked for it was quite smelly. I particularly hated it when I had to go after dark. This happened occasionally, and it seemed a long way down the sloping concrete ramp and across the grass to the toilet. When the wind blew it rustled and moved the row of trees near the falling-down fence causing it to make a creaking noise. I was always frightened and I worried especially that the night man might come when I was on the toilet at night, and then he would see my bare bottom. Sometimes a chook chose to roost in there for the night, and a couple of times I sat on one setting us both off squawking. I was very glad when the sewerage went through in our street and we got an inside toilet with a chain.

Behind the high fence and row of trees was a large area of grass. Sometimes Dad grew vegetables in part of this land, and I remember one year when he had a bumper crop of tomatoes. In retrospect I think this may have been Dad's attempt at what was called a Victory Garden. During the war years people were being encouraged to grow their own vegetables because commercial canned goods were needed for the troops. There was also a shortage of labour to transport fruit and vegetables to the markets.

I actually don't remember Dad growing any other vegetables but he was certainly very successful with his tomatoes. A lot of them ripened at the same time, and we girls helped pick them and carried them up to the house in our pinnies until the big pine table in the kitchen finished up covered by them. It must have been a huge job for Mum to preserve them all, because this was before we had a refrigerator and Mum would have had to bottle all those tomatoes. Perhaps she gave a lot of them away because neighbours often shared excess produce during the war years.

Dad was an erratic gardener though and I don't remember him showing an interest in gardening again until he retired. At that time he built a glass house in the backyard of the house in Tower Road and grew enormously tall and productive Grosse Lisse tomatoes and potted up cuttings. He also grew some vegetables in the garden including huge marrows. I couldn't convince him that they were now called zucchinis and were meant to be picked when only about six inches long. For Dad it was the bigger the better.

All this was in the future and after the year of the tomatoes the back yard at Windsor Street reverted to a place of rough grass and weeds with the odd bush here and there and blackberries along the back fence. This was where Jane and I played schools when we were little and other chasing games when our brothers were older.

At the bottom of the block next door was a row of pine trees. These trees weren't radiata pines or the other more spreading kind you see on fence lines or surrounding houses in the country. Both of these varieties have sharp dark-green needles, but our pine trees had soft lighter green needles. The branches spread out sideways and the tops of the trees were almost flat.

Jane and I spent hours playing in these trees with our young brothers, Jack and his sister Pat and the two Smith boys Johnny and Brian. We eight kids spent a lot of time together and considered ourselves a gang.

When we played in the pine trees we'd try to climb from one end of the row to the other without touching the ground. We had races doing this and the person who won got to choose which tree was theirs for the day. You could make nests or houses in the tops of many of them, but there was one that was particularly good. When you won the race you always picked that one, and chose someone to share it with you. During the football season we all perched in our tree houses and watched the game being played on the oval across the paddock. I don't think any of us really followed the games and certainly didn't know the rules of play, but we knew people paid to go and watch the football so felt we were getting something for free.

The paddock between these trees and the oval sometimes had cows in it, but when the cows were taken elsewhere we played wars there. Kids who went to Glenorchy School also played in this area, and if they came when we were there we fought them. I think we considered it a sort of no-man's land between our territory and theirs. It was a flat paddock with numerous briar bushes dotted around it and cow dung lying all over the place. Each group gathered up as much dung as they could and then threw it at the other kids from hiding places behind the briar bushes. We accompanied our throws with insults. They cried out, 'Moonah mugs eat slugs.' Our war cry was, 'Glenorchy germs eat worms.' No one ever got hurt so it was fairly harmless fun, but we must have been very stinky little kids at the end of the day.

The paddock at the top of the street was enormous and empty except for the school inspector's house. We were fairly scared of all school inspectors, who came once a year to check on how we were going with our schoolwork. At least that's what the teachers told us, and it wasn't until I joined the profession that I discovered they were really assessing the teachers. Anyhow we steered clear of the school inspector's house and land, but we still had lots of space in which to roam.

One of these was the avenue, which was a beautiful laneway where we often played. It must have led to a house, but we didn't ever see anyone in the avenue or any cars going up or down it. We knew it must belong to someone though because on either side were plants you normally only saw in people's gardens. There were lilac and rose bushes, and lovely trees that had chains of yellow flowers hanging down on them in the spring. Mum told me they were laburnum trees. There were also quite a lot of almond trees that had gorgeous blossom in spring, and then in the autumn we'd sometimes find the nuts lying on the ground.

It was a lovely place to play, and one day Jane and I were there with John and Roger. We girls were climbing the trees and the boys were playing underneath. I didn't see what happened to the boys, but a man suddenly appeared under my tree and offered to help me climb. He put his hand on my leg, but I moved out of his reach and said I didn't need any help. Jane and I were wearing new shorts that had bibs with frills that went over our shoulders. Later Jane told us what the man had done when he was pretending to help her climb her tree. At the time I was happily climbing my tree, then suddenly Mum appeared and the man ran away. She was very red in the face, for she must have run all the way up the street, across the paddock and into the avenue. Evidently the man had told John and Roger to get lost, and John had had enough sense to run home and tell Mum about the nasty man. My youngest sister Val would have been a baby at that time so Mum must have left her with the woman next door and then run like the wind fearing her little girls were in danger. After we came down from our trees she asked us what the man done, and I said nothing to me because I didn't need help to climb. Jane said he had put his hand up the leg of her shorts and inside her panties and that was when Mum had arrived.

After that event surprisingly we were still allowed to play in the avenue, but Mum warned us to be wary of strangers and not to let anyone touch us. We didn't go there after that unless the whole gang was playing together, and I don't think I loved it quite as much after our meeting with the nasty man. I wasn't sure what he had been trying to do, but this event added to my fear of Robert and Dennis the following year. I didn't know why they wanted to pull down my pants, but knew it was wrong.

Despite this encounter we were still allowed to wander freely.

It was at this time that we began joining or forming clubs. Jane and I joined the Girls' Friendly Society and also the Gould's Bird League. Jack joined this too and we went to meetings after school to learn how to identify birds and not to touch a nest if it had eggs in it. For a while we were the friends of all birds, but then a plover attacked Jack while we were walking through a paddock. It swooped down and clawed his head making it bleed. From then on we weren't so sure about our new-found friends and dropped out of the league.

We next formed what we called the Discovery Club and ranged the paddocks searching for treasures. While we were playing this game we found a sledge under a briar bush, and felt very pleased with ourselves. For several weeks we played with this sledge, sliding on it down a sloping side of the paddock. You had to turn quickly when you neared the bottom or you could finish up in a barbed-wire fence but it was tremendous fun while you were in motion. After playing with the sledge we always put it back under the briar bush where we'd found it. We were very upset when it disappeared, but I think we really knew that it must have belonged to some other kids.

On another occasion our gang was pretending to be in an Explorers Club and went further than usual, across the paddock and past the quarry and the avenue until we found a beautiful orchard. In retrospect I think that orchard was probably part of the land my grandfather had farmed and where our mother had spent many happy childhood hours but this didn't occur to me at the time. The day we chanced upon it was very hot and summery and the air was alive with the sound of bees humming. There were orange and brown butterflies filling the air and bright pink, purple and white flowers, that we called pincushions, covered the ground under the trees. For us rather fey children it was the way we had imagined fairyland would be.

There were still some little red apples hanging on the trees so we ate some, lying in a shady spot on a bed of green twining leaves with purple flowers growing amongst them. When we finished our apples we ate some of these purple flowers and cleaned our teeth with a little white bit we pulled from the middle of them. Strangely enough we all went to sleep, and woke up feeling as though we had somehow been enchanted. Perhaps we had been poisoned slightly, because I later learnt that the plant we ate was convolvulus and it is considered poisonous.

Probably our most favourite place in which to play was the quarry. This was where Auntie Ron's ex-husband and the other men played two-up on Sunday mornings. It was very steep on two sides and had more gentle slopes on the other two. The more gentle sides were covered in yellow daisy bushes and we made houses for ourselves amongst the flowers. We also scrambled up the steep slopes, pretending to be mountain climbers.

The rest of the quarry was flat and smooth but in the centre there was a deep hole that was always full of dark, sludgy-looking water. When the sun shone on the water we could make out strange shapes at the bottom. Jack thought it was a car that had been driven in there accidentally, and that perhaps there was a skeleton or two hidden in those murky depths. I didn't think this was likely because the shapes didn't look as big as a car. Nevertheless Jane and I frightened our younger brothers about what might be at the bottom of this hole so that they wouldn't go too close, for we knew it would be dangerous to fall in.

Apart from this slightly dangerous part of the quarry the places where we played were safe. I'm so glad that I grew up in a world where there were so many lovely places in which to wander; a world where children could run free and parents felt we were not in too much danger.

Most of our weekends were spent out of doors, but when I was about seven Shirl, Jane and I began going to the pictures on some Saturday afternoons. The Montrose

Picture Theatre was on the Main Road about half a mile from our street. We were each given nine pennies to spend, sixpence to get into the pictures and three pence for sweets. The three of us always bought a pink stick, which was musk, a green peppermint stick, and a yellow stick which was made of barley sugar. We kept that one till last because it lasted the longest.

The picture theatre was really just a weatherboard shed and the seats were long wooden benches with backs to them. Nothing very glamorous about that, but to us it was a magic place.

There were always two pictures and a serial and sometimes cartoons as well. From memory a lot of the films were westerns or about the war, but there were also comedies and musicals. The musicals were our favourites and so were the women who starred in them. Jane and I loved Carmen Miranda and thought Betty Grable the most beautiful woman in the world. We were most impressed when we learnt that her legs were insured for a million dollars, even though we didn't really understand what this insurance thing meant.

When we both got bikes we'd ride out to a place called 'The Chalet' in Claremont, which is an outer suburb of Hobart. The Chalet was a rather lovely big house at the top of a beautiful garden. I think grownups went there for lunch, but there was a little shop at the front where Jane and I bought ice creams. We then sat on a swinging seat that had a flowered canopy over the top. We thought this swing the height of glamour and sat there, idly swinging while we ate ice creams and imagined we were Betty Grable and Carmen Miranda.

After musicals our favourites were the serials. I don't remember what they were about, but I know each episode finished with the goodies in some ghastly predicament. We'd wait anxiously through the week wondering how they could survive. Once they were trapped in a room with the water rising around them. Another time they were locked in a cage full of venomous snakes. It didn't matter how dire their predicament was each week the goodies miraculously escaped and lived to fight another day. This still didn't stop us worrying about them but I guess that was part of the excitement.

The films were what I think were called reel to reel, and the projectionist sat up high above us in a little room and projected the film onto the screen at the front of the hall. Sometimes the film would break and we were left in complete darkness. If it wasn't very long before the film came back on we all sat there quietly, but if it took a long time everyone started stamping their feet, slow clapping and calling out. There would be a terrible din and it was a relief when the film recommenced.

The War Years

I have only mentioned the war in passing, but I grew up with a strong awareness of its existence.

I was only two when war broke out. Evidently Dad tried to join up, but because he worked at the Zinc Works and they were producing munitions he was turned down. The work there was classed as an essential service. I think he was very disappointed, but Mum was upset that he'd even tried to go when he had family responsibilities. They had one of their rare arguments about this, but I don't know whether I remember this or whether Mum told me later how angry she'd been with him.

Because our father wasn't fighting the war didn't worry me much until Dad built the shelter shed. It was really just a hole in the ground, down in the yard near the falling down fence. It was quite large because it had to be big enough to hold Mum and Dad and five kids. There were steps cut in the earth leading down to the hole and a board over the top of it that was supposed to keep out the rain, but didn't.

I had only ever seen one other shelter shed and that was Auntie Ella's. Her husband Roy was alive then, and although they weren't any relation to us we called them uncle and auntie. They had no children of their own and seemed to quite like us visiting. I didn't like their house much because it smelt of their old dog and musty newspapers that filled one room. I did, however, like their garden for it was very neat, with vegetables growing in rows and a lovely shady part near the back door that was full of ferns. Best of all though was their shelter shed. Sometimes Auntie Ella let Jane and me play in it, but we had to be careful not to break anything.

This shelter shed was roofed over properly, soil was placed on top and flowers were planted in the soil. Auntie Ella said this was to camouflage it if planes flew over. Because of the sturdy roof and soil layer it didn't get wet inside the way ours did. Inside there was linoleum on the floor and a little table and chairs. Along one wall were shelves stocked with tinned food and water bottles and on the table was a candle in a holder and some matches. It all looked rather like a toy house so of course we girls loved it.

Our shelter shed was a very sorry thing by comparison, and from seeing Auntie Ella's one I knew ours didn't come up to scratch. Would we be safe in it, and what about supplies of food and water?

From the time our shelter shed was built until the end of the war I had frequent nightmares about being in there and the Germans coming. I must have seen photos of German soldiers in the newspapers, for I knew what they looked like. In my nightmares they were either marching through our back yard with their bayonets poking out in front of them ready to stab us, or else they were somewhere near and I was trying desperately to get back up to the house to get food because I was hungry. I don't know what Freud would make of these nightmares, but I know I didn't like going to bed at all through those years because of them.

I remember telling Shirl how much I hated going to bed and her saying, 'I love bed.' I wanted to tell her about my nightmares but thought she'd think me silly or over imaginative.

During the War Years most factories were busy producing goods and arms for the war effort. This meant that few factory-made toys were available so many toys were home-made or second hand. I know the bike I was given for my eighth birthday was second hand, but it had been repainted and had a new chain. It was as good as new as far as I was concerned.

Except for my Donald Duck, I don't remember any other home-made toys I had, but I think the boys had wooden trucks or trains made by Dad. Despite the shortage of toys during those years we each always had a pillow-case full of goodies at Christmas. Usually we received only one special present each, so the pillow-cases were bulked up with clothes, things like pencils and drawing books and lollies. Although this was meagre fare compared with what children get today we looked forward to Christmas mornings, and were pleased with what we got.

I remember getting a doll one year and I thought her quite beautiful. Her body was made of material but she had a very pretty china head. Unfortunately I didn't have her for very long because Roger, who was a toddler at the time, accidentally knocked her off my bed and her face smashed when she hit the floor. I know I was terribly upset about this and cried. Mum gathered up the pieces and said she could mend her. She must have spent a long time fitting and gluing the head together, but I wasn't happy with the end result. I could still see little cracks in her face and she was no longer beautiful. After that I didn't play with her any more. It seems, what with my kewpie doll having to be left in the hospital and now a doll I loved being damaged, I didn't have much luck with dolls.

Mum always said the hardest thing for her about the war was the rationing. From the time I was about five, several basic foodstuffs were rationed including meat, tea, butter and sugar. Because Dad went hunting for rabbits and kangaroos and did quite a lot of fishing the rationing of meat was not a big problem. Mum made the most delicious kangaroo patties by mincing the roo meat with carrots, breadcrumbs and bacon. With the tail she made kangaroo tail soup that she flavoured with vegemite. We also had lots of stews and mince dishes and lambs fry fairly regularly. Mum called it velvet steak, obviously to make it sound more appealing, and we all loved it. Another favourite was toad-in-the-hole; a dish of sausages cooked in a light golden batter and slathered with tomato sauce. This was a good dish for a large family as it made a few sausages go a long way.

Grandma brought us dairy butter that she made. This was always rather salty and we didn't like it as much as ordinary butter, but it must have helped eke out the limited amount Mum could buy with her ration book. Because Grandma and Pop owned a milk bar, and made their own ice cream, they were allocated a generous allowance of milk and sugar. We benefited from this, as they brought a bag of sugar most Sundays, besides the other goodies. The extra sugar and butter supplied by Grandma enabled Mum to continue cooking the kiss biscuits and buttery cakes we all enjoyed. This was not the case in many homes and recipes for cakes and biscuits that used less of these precious ingredients were exchanged between housewives wishing to provide something sweet for their children. I remember Shirl coming home from school and telling us a friend of hers said her mother made a cake that was eggless, sugarless and butterless. We joked about this saying it must also have been tasterless. We couldn't imagine it having much taste, although I do have fond memories of suet puddings like jam roly-poly and steamed golden syrup pudding as being delicious and they used neither butter nor sugar. Tea was probably a bit of a problem for our mother for she loved her cup of tea and the allowance per person was very small at ½ a pound for five weeks. This is equal to about 240 grams, the amount I drink in two weeks.

The hardest thing for Mum was the rationing of clothes. I remember her saying that it barely covered our school uniforms so she had to make most of our clothes. She enjoyed sewing and was good at it, but some of our clothes were pretty daggy. The overcoats we all wore when we were young weren't exactly glamorous, but we did have some pretty dresses.

Occasionally we had store bought clothes, and one of my favourites was the little outfit that consisted of a pleated skirt in very fine wool with a matching top that I wore on my first trip into town. We three girls all had the same except mine was blue, Jane's red and Shirl's green. The problem with being the third girl was that I got hand-me-downs. For years I wore these outfits, first mine that I loved, then Jane's and finally I grew into Shirl's. By that time I was heartily sick of them and never wanted to see another pleated skirt again.

By far the worst clothes any and all of us wore were our bathers. Obviously Mum couldn't make bathers, but she certainly found some that lasted. I think they were usually made of light wool which meant they soon lost what little shape they'd had to begin with and drooped unbecomingly from our shoulders. One of my sisters has a photo of Shirl in a particularly odd pair of bathers with a large fish decorating the top of them. Many years later they turn up again in a photo, this time on Roger and looking a bit the worse for wear. The three of us in between probably all wore them also. Other bathers were nearly as bad and long-lived. I think I had the same pair of woollen bathers from the time I was ten until I was thirteen or fourteen, when I finally got a beautiful aqua satin pair. I loved them inordinately for they even had shaping at the bust, although I had precious little to put into the bra cups.

Petrol being rationed was what affected Dad the most. He drove to work every day, to Tech two or three nights a week and to umpire football matches or to go fishing or hunting at weekends. From about 1941 we also started going to Connellys Marsh for the holidays and that was quite a long trip. With all this traipsing around he would have used quite a lot of petrol.

I have vague memories of Dad building a contraption that produced steam and was somehow meant to help drive the car, but I have no idea whether or not it worked. I do remember clearly, however, that when we were going on a long trip Dad turned off the engine and coasted down any hills we came to. We knew it was against the law and were frightened a policeman would see Dad doing this. It was always a relief when we came to the bottom of the hill and he turned the engine back on again.

There weren't a lot of cars around during those years. Dad and the school inspector who lived in solitary splendour across the paddock were the only people in our street who had cars. When the school inspector drove past we hid, because we were frightened of him, even when he was in his big black car.

Just about the only other cars that we saw regularly were delivery vans. We'd drop Mum's order into the grocery shop at the bottom of the street on the way to school. The grocer made his deliveries once a week in a little van and always put in a bag of boiled lollies for free. We also left Mum's meat order with the butcher twice a week, and he delivered it or we picked it up on our way home. Bread was delivered every day and so was milk, but our milkman used a horse and cart. When he pulled up Mum would run out with her biggest pot. He'd fill it up, scooping out the milk from a silvery container with a sort of shovel made of metal. Mum boiled the milk and left it in the pot to cool down. A thick layer of cream settled on top and we often had this on bread and jam as an after school snack before heading outside to play.

We had occasional visits from other men in carts. There was the man who came round with a load of fresh scallops in his cart during the scallop season. Mum always bought several scoopfuls of scallops from him. I remember hoping she'd do them all in batter and not ruin them by putting them in curry, but she invariably cooked them both ways.

There was also a rabbiter who sometimes came around in a cart, ringing a little bell and calling out 'Rabbio', and a man who came in a van on Sundays but only during the winter. He sold oranges and crumpets. This now seems a strange combination but I think crumpets may have only been made during the cold weather in those days, and oranges are at their best and cheapest during our winter. After a visit from this man for tea we always had crumpets toasted by the fire in the front parlour on long toasting forks followed by oranges. These Sundays were the only time we used the parlour as a family.

Another salesman who came to our door was the Rawleighs Man, but I don't think he drove a car. I'm fairly sure he walked, carrying a large suitcase in each hand. Our man was named Ron, and Mum had known him when they were children. He was a tall gangly man with a twitch in one eye and legs that jiggled when he sat having a cup of tea after showing Mum his wares. I loved seeing him open the cases that had secret compartments to hold all the different things he had for sale. Mum always bought something from him, usually vanilla essence or an ointment that seemed to heal everything.

After he left Mum would look after him sadly and say, 'Poor Ron,' and put the new bottle of vanilla essence in the pantry, next to others already there.

I asked her one day why he twitched and jiggled and she said he had bad nerves because he had been in the war. Then I felt sorry for him too.

When the war ended we had a school assembly in the middle of the day and were told that the war had ended and to celebrate we were all allowed to go home early. Jane and I were walking up our street when some aeroplanes flew over. We knew they were our planes because they made big letters in the sky to show we had won. I think the letters were V E for Victory in Europe and the flight was to verify and celebrate the end of the war, but being overly dramatic kids we pretended the planes belonged to the Germans. We ran for cover, and crept up the side of the road where there were some bushes to shield us from the evil pilots. Mum thought we were just excited about the war ending when we rushed in red-faced and sweaty. She didn't know we'd spent the past half hour dodging and weaving and hiding from enemy aircraft.

Religion

Besides the aunts in their cars the only visitors we had who came in a car were Grandma and Pop. They always visited on Sunday mornings, and would be there when Shirl, Jane and I arrived home from Sunday school.

I don't know where Sunday school was held, but I remember being in a big room with the little kids while my sisters were somewhere else. This didn't bother me because I liked the things we did in our room.

We little kids sat in rows on the floor while the teacher told us a story. She had a board and lots of little cut out shapes of people and animals and scenery, things like palm trees and sand dunes. These were made of felt and stuck to the board where she placed them. While she told the story she put the different shapes on the board to illustrate what she was saying. I clearly remember enjoying her story of baby Jesus being born, and watching entranced as she moved the three wise men across the board on their camels until they came to the manger where Jesus was lying in a crib. I can't imagine kids today finding this very exciting, but picture books were a rarity and television and computer games were still things of future. For me these illustrated stories were fascinating.

When the story was finished we all stood up and formed a circle and sang songs. We sang 'Jesus bids us shine with a pure clear light', and, 'Jesus loves the little children, all the children of the world'. Our last song was always, 'All things bright and beautiful, all creatures great and small'. This was my very favourite song for I liked the words about the glowing flowers and the birds' tiny wings.

After Sunday school finished I'd meet up again with my sisters for the walk home. We knew Grandma and Pop would be there by the time we got home, and used to jump up on the little concrete humps that crossed the gutter to see who could spot Pop's car first. We enjoyed their visits because Mum made scones and kiss biscuits or cake for morning tea. They also always brought things with them from the shop. Besides the butter that Grandma made, there would be slightly overripe bananas and oranges Grandma called specks because they were also very ripe and sometimes had tiny specks of brown on them. Evidently these fruits were too ripe to sell but I really enjoyed them and still like bananas and oranges best when they are a bit overripe.

On Sunday evenings the Salvation Army people often came and sang in our street. They wore navy uniforms with red trimming and the ladies wore funny hats. They stood under a street light while they banged on a big drum and shook their tambourines and sang. The main song I remember them singing is, 'Onward Christian Soldiers', but they must have sung others. We were allowed to lean out the front window and listen to them until they finished their singing and marched off down the street. After we closed the window and went to our bedroom we could still hear the sounds of the drum and their marching feet echoing in the night air.

I thought it looked a rather fun religion. Mum said they were very good people and that they did a lot for our men who were fighting in the war. I pictured them marching around the places where the war was going on, singing and playing to cheer up the soldiers. I wondered if God looked after them because they were good, and hoped He did.

Many years later I read of how they were indeed often close to the fighting, not marching and singing around the trenches but providing food and hot drinks and comfort to the soldiers. As an adult I occasionally saw members of the

Salvation Army in the hotels, wandering in those smoke-filled rooms chatting cheerfully to drunken men, selling their paper the "War Cry" and rattling tins for donations. Evidently their work during the wars was well known because they were treated with respect and never hassled by the drinkers. When I saw them in these noisy, riotous surroundings I thought them heroic. I would buy their paper but discard it guiltily in a bin at the first opportunity, for by then I was no longer a believer.

Another early brush with religion was through the Girls' Friendly Society. As I have mentioned earlier this was run by Miss Kippax after school, and Jane and I joined up when I was in grade four and Jane in grade five. She told us bible stories, and also talked about how we should help our fellow man. I thought this a strange way of saying to be helpful to other people because I knew she meant other kids and ladies as well, but she did sometimes have an old fashioned way of saying things.

When Miss Kippax told us about a camp that was being organised by the society Jane and I wanted to go. Mum said we could, and we were given a list of the things we needed to take. We had sort of duffle bags in which we packed our clothes and toiletries and we were each given a little bit of spending money. I seem to remember that we also had to take certain items of food but I don't remember what. This was in 1947 so perhaps some things were still rationed or scarce.

Dad took us to where a bus was waiting and we climbed on board. We had never been away from home before except for staying with relatives when Mum had a baby, so for us this was quite an adventure.

The camp was somewhere in Conningham, a little beachside suburb. When we arrived we were shown to the big room where we would sleep and we chose our beds and put our bags on them. We then all gathered in a big room and were welcomed by Miss Kippax and another lady. They told us what we would be doing, where we would have our meals and that we would all doss in and have a jolly time.

Well we did have a jolly time. We had prayers and stories from the bible, but we also went to the little beach to build sand castles and paddle in the water as well as playing chasings and hide-and-seek among the trees in the grounds of the camp. We were allowed to go to a nearby shop, and there we bought lollies for a midnight feast.

There was a roster for helping prepare the vegetables and another for washing up, but we didn't mind this because the kitchen ladies were nice and the meals good. On the Sunday we walked to a little stone church that was nearby. It was really lovely inside with beautiful stained glass windows and there was lots of blossom in big copper jars near the altar and around the church. I thought it quite beautiful, and felt uplifted by my surroundings although I have no memory of the service.

On the final day Miss Kippax came up to me and said, 'Have you let the Lord into your heart Barbara?'

I had never heard this expression before and felt uncomfortable at the thought of sharing my body with anyone, even the Lord, so I said, 'No Miss Kippax.'

She just said something like, 'That's a pity,' and didn't bother me any further.

When Jane was asked she was as baffled as I by the expression but thought it easier to say she had. She told Miss Kippax she had let the Lord into her heart, and as a result was given a long talk about how much better she would now feel.

For a week after this camp Jane was indeed different because as she said, 'She was saved.' She did my turn of the washing up which was great as far as I was concerned and well worth not being saved. Apart from doing this chore for me she was such a goody-goody and so holier than thou I thought her quite unbearable. I was glad when she decided it was too hard imagining she had the Lord in her heart all the time and went back to being normal.

We had another stab at getting religion when we were in our early teens. At Mum's instigation we went to confirmation classes. We had been christened as babies but now we would be prepared to become true members of the church. The minister had two sons roughly the same ages as Jane and me and we sat together during the lessons. They were quite naughty boys and their father was a very boring speaker who sprinkled his talk with lots of pauses which he filled in with ums. We four spent most of the time counting how many times the reverend gentleman said um and I think we sometimes got up to over a hundred. Needless to say we didn't take any notice of what he was actually telling us.

On confirmation day we dressed in new white frocks and were duly made members of the church. We attended occasionally and helped decorate the church one Palm Sunday. That was rather fun, but slowly we became complete atheists as we grew up. Mum was always disappointed that none of us really believed in God and I felt I'd let her down. When I talked to her about my feelings she said, 'What you need to do is recognise the force within you that makes you strong.'

I have found those words of my mother's more comforting and strengthening than any belief in an unseen and unimaginable God.

At the Beach

Although I don't believe in an all-powerful God I have retained an almost childlike wonder and reverence for the natural world. The stunning beauty of a sunset, the intricate patterning on a flower, the energy of waves crashing onto rocks and the magic to be felt in the damp earth smells and rioting greens of a rainforest fill me with joy and lift my soul. I don't, however, feel the need to attribute all this glory to a God.

The freedom to roam that I enjoyed as a child fostered these feelings, and the place that has given me a continuing tie to the natural world and all its wonders has been Connellys Marsh. As I write this I can look up from my computer and see the same gumtree covered hill I first saw when I was four years old, or walk out my front door and see the crescent-shaped beach where I played with my siblings more than seventy-five years ago.

I was four the first time we camped at Connellys. Dad and his great mate Narna had found this place while on a fishing trip and decided to bring their young families here for a holiday. My main memory of that first year is that the men set up two tents. One was smallish, and Mum, my little brother and the baby were to sleep in there with Narna's wife Mildred and their two little girls. The other tent was enormous, and this was where the cooking and eating would take place and also where the men and the remaining children would sleep. I thought this was great and truly exciting, but then it was decided I was perhaps too young to sleep in the tent and should bed down in the front of Narna's car that was parked near the women's tent.

I'm sure I made a fuss about this for I had been looking forward to sleeping in that big tent. Whatever fuss I made was to no avail, for I was banished to Narna's car for all that holiday, much to my disgust. I remember being quite pleased when Jane wet herself in the bed she was sharing with Dad, for I knew I wouldn't have done that.

That is the only bad memory of the first time of camping at Connellys. The rest are of days of joy. None of us could swim so we weren't allowed to go into the sea, but there was a lagoon where a stream ran down to the sand and here we spent our days. I'm sure every day was warm and sunny, for we spent all our time in this lagoon or making sandcastles on its banks. During the day we ate sandwiches Mum and Mildred prepared, and at night we sat around a camp fire eating the fish Dad and Narna had caught.

For the next few years we spent a week or two camping at the beach each summer holiday but things changed when Dad built our shack and Narna built one next door. From then on we spent virtually all of the summer school holidays there, only returning to civilization in time to be outfitted with new school uniforms and to buy our books. We also went there at Easter time and for the other school holidays.

Getting ready to go to the shack took a long time and was quite a business, for we needed to take clothes, food and pillows for two adults, five children and one baby. Fitting everything into the car and still leaving room for everyone must have been a work of art. Even though we'd start packing quite early it would still be mid-morning before we were ready to go.

At that time Hobart still had the floating bridge and Dad had to stop the car and pay a toll before we could continue on our journey. I think there were times when some of us kids hid under pillows on the floor of the car so that it cost less. None of my siblings remember doing this, so either I just thought this would be a fun thing to do so imagined it, or else they don't like to admit to our parents encouraging us to break the law.

Once we were safely across the floating bridge we drove along a winding road and then there was a long straight stretch. On the left was the aerodrome and we looked out eagerly to see if we could see any planes. After this we crossed over two causeways and drove into the town of Sorell. By this time we would all be hot and travel-weary from being cramped in the back of the car. Dad always stopped there to buy us ice cream cones, a real treat in those days when few houses were blessed with refrigerators.

Jane was prone to carsickness. When she started turning a whitish-green shade, a sure sign that she was feeling unwell the rest of us would say, 'Buttered toast and creamy cocoa,' in quiet sly voices that Mum and Dad couldn't hear. The very thought of this food and drink combination was guaranteed to increase the turmoil in her stomach. Soon Dad would have to stop the car so she could get out and vomit at the side of the road. When this happened we felt sorry for her, but our regrets weren't strong enough to prevent us repeating this behaviour on subsequent trips. Kids can be so mean, even to those they love.

Once we had passed Sorell the road became very twisty and there were several hilly parts. During the war years when petrol was rationed it was on this part of the journey that Dad turned off the engine and let the car freewheel down the hills. As I have mentioned earlier, I worried that a policeman would catch him doing this, and was always relieved when we reached the bottom of a hill and Dad restarted the engine.

The highway was sealed but once we reached the turnoff the road was gravel and not very well maintained so Dad drove slowly. I loved this part of the trip. The road was lined with gum trees that created patterns of light and shade on the gravel. Through the trees you could catch glimpses of paddocks full of sheep and distant purple hills. Far to the right you could see an expanse of shimmering blue water and near the roadway was a small rounded hill. Dad always told us this had been one of the signal points used when messages were sent from Port Arthur to Hobart during the convict era. We didn't mind him repeating himself about this because we knew when we reached there we didn't have much further to go.

After we wound down the hill and across the little wooden bridge over the Carlton River Dad would stop at the farmhouse near the river to get the key to the gate. The farmer who lived there owned all the land at Connellys Marsh and Dad leased the piece on which he'd built our shack. The whole area was fenced and we needed the key to unlock the gate so we could get in.

Dad always talked to the farmer for absolute ages while we kids fidgeted and complained in the crowded back seat of the car. Sometimes Mum took pity on us and let the oldest of us walk the last couple of miles. We'd race each other up the road, trying to be first to reach the top of the rise and get the first view of the beach. That view of the white sand curving in a perfect crescent, the aqua water shading to darkest blue and the distant low hills was a magical sight.

If we arrived at the gate before the car we searched for flowers at the side of the road. We particularly liked a plant Dad called sags. He said it was a weed but to us they looked like orchids and we thought them very beautiful. If we found any we carried them carefully until we reached the shack, then put them in a glass jar on the table in the kitchen.

When Dad drove up and unlocked the gate we'd get back into the car for the tortuous drive through the marsh. The way in was a dank sandy track winding around big gum trees and across moist hollows filled with logs that had been placed there on previous trips through this quagmire to the shack. Sometimes we had to drag more logs and bracken across these spots before we could proceed. Getting to the place where we had camped had been easier because we'd skirted along the side of this swamp, but the shack was built near the middle of the beach and much of the marsh had to be crossed to reach it.

Eventually we would arrive at the clearing and there it would be, its tin sides crackling in the heat. We'd scramble from the car throw off our shoes and race into the water. After Dad built a small boat shed on the beach John and I used to clamber onto its roof and jump from the front of it onto the sand. We did this to show off because no-one else was brave enough to do it for the roof sloped up so it was about three metres off the ground.

By the time the shack was built my two older sisters and I could swim, a skill we had acquired during one of the many Sunday drives we went on. These started after Grandma was widowed and I think were meant to be a treat for her. We kids didn't mind them even though we had to be on our best behaviour when she was around. We usually ended up in some pretty place for a picnic lunch and one day it was in a spot next to the Jordan River. It was a very hot day and the water looked inviting so Dad said we could go into the water. We girls stripped off all our clothes and went in and magically found we could dog paddle in the almost still, deep water. From then on we swam in the sea at Connellys, gradually progressing to breast stroke and learning to float on our backs. Some years later the boys still couldn't swim and didn't seem interested in learning so one day Dad and Narna pretended to be giving them piggyback rides then took them into deep water and let them drop. Both boys then dogpaddled back to shore but I can't say it was a very successful way of teaching kids to swim. Neither John nor Roger ever swam much as kids and I don't remember seeing either of them swimming as adults. In contrast we girls loved swimming and it is still one of my greatest joys.

Dad and Narna built the first shacks at Connellys Marsh and for the first few years our two families were the only ones there. Narna's shack was a small timber, two-roomed dwelling but ours was larger, with a concrete floor, timber framework, tin cladding on the bedroom walls and weatherboards on the kitchen. Getting all the materials for the two shacks across the marshlands must have been quite a business, but we kids knew nothing about this. All we knew was that one year we were camping in tents and the next we had this wonderful place where we could stay for weeks.

Our shack consisted of three rooms, the girls' room, the boys' room and the kitchen. You entered straight into the kitchen that had a table and chairs, a couch under the window and an open fireplace. Leading from the kitchen was a short passage with the boys' room on the right and the girls' room at the end. This was the largest, a long room with windows along one wall and a door to the outside. We girls slept in a row on single iron beds and Mum slept in a double bed with our baby sister Val. When our baby brother Bernard was born Val graduated to an iron bed. Dad, John and Roger slept in the boys' room which was much smaller.

In the clearing outside the shack was a fire pit with a tripod to hold the big camp oven and leading away from there was a pathway to the outside dunny. This was a small, dark structure that smelt strongly of a mixture of a strong chemical and shit. To avoid using this uninviting place we kids usually peed in the bushes and only used the dunny for number twos.

Next to the tank, which was close to the shack, was a tin dish on a box. This was our bathroom. We bathed in the sea every day so tank water was only used for washing faces, hands and sandy feet and for cleaning our teeth.

Beyond the clearing was the marshland. Dad was convinced that this marshy land was teeming with snakes so we were banned from going there. Actually we didn't find the marshes very appealing as we travelled through them on our way to the beach so didn't mind this restriction. Being imaginative kids Jane and I conjured up strange and mysterious creatures that lived among the fallen trees and rank ferns. We turned our backs on these ominous creatures and looked to the sea and sand. For the four weeks of our summer holiday and for shorter periods of time throughout the year our lives revolved around playing on the sand, swimming in the sea and fishing.

I don't think camping or shack life really appealed to Narna's wife Mildred. She seemed to be constantly worrying about whether her two little daughters were clean, and she didn't enjoy being on the sand or in the sea the way our mother did. After a short time Narna sold his shack. The people who bought it didn't use it much, so most of the time we had the place to ourselves and felt it all belonged to us.

Jane and I claimed great tracts of foreshore and pretended we were wealthy plantation owners growing valuable crops of marram grass. Small sand islands were exposed when the tide went out. We would each stake out an island, decorate it with branches and rushes and repel others from coming on our land. Shirl didn't play any of these imaginative games with us, but John and Roger joined in with this one.

We had no electricity so everything was cooked over the fire inside or outside in the fire pit. Cooked meat and other perishables like milk and butter were kept in a Coolgardie safe that hung in the little passage off the boys' room. Lanterns were our only form of lighting so evenings were spent in the kitchen or outside around the fire. When you were tired you felt your way to bed in the dark.

Dad had bought a lot of army surplus stuff to set up the shack. The iron beds we slept on had once presumably graced an army barracks. I think our mattresses were just hessian palliasses filled with ferns instead of straw. We didn't use sheets at the shack, but slept under scratchy grey blankets which had also once been used by soldiers. We brought our pillows from home so at least we had something soft and smooth beneath our heads. All this sounds extremely primitive and uncomfortable, but we slept soundly after days in the open air.

The kitchen utensils were also army surplus stock. We ate off tin dishes that were white with a blue edge and drank tea sweetened with condensed milk from tin mugs decorated in the same basic way.

We lived like peasants but ate like kings.

While Dad was with us we went fishing every day. Jane remembers our father as being very strict when we were in the boat; in fact she says he turned into a virtual Captain Bligh. I actually don't remember him being particularly bossy or strict at these times. In retrospect it can't have been easy having four or five young kids out fishing with you in a dinghy. He had to row the dingy and later when he had an outboard motor stop and start the engine when the boat needed repositioning. He also needed to help the younger ones get their fish off the hooks. When we were older we had to do that for ourselves, and he taught us to stab the flathead in between their eyes and to be careful of their spikes.

Often we caught dozens of fish, so we were also taught how to clean them at an early age. Dad actually tried to implement a rule whereby you cleaned what you caught, but the boys tired of this job quickly and Shirl wasn't that interested in fishing so often Jane and I finished up helping him do most of the cleaning.

After the fish were cleaned Mum rolled them in flour and cooked them in a big, black cast iron pan, either over the open fire in the kitchen or at the fire pit. Often we each ate as many as four or five fish at a sitting.

On still nights when the water was calm Dad went floundering. We kids were not allowed to go with him because we wouldn't be quiet enough and would frighten the fish away. Instead we all sat up playing cards until it was time for him to go. We'd troop down to the beach to see him off with his spear, a light and the small punt he had made to hold the battery and the fish he would catch.

We would watch until his stocky figure disappeared in the gloom and we could only see a distant reflection of the light in the calm water. Sometimes I lay awake worrying about him out there in that dark expanse all by himself, but he was always safely with us in the morning. Usually there were flounder for breakfast, cooked outside and eaten in the morning sunlight.

Dad had quite a collection of craypots and cray rings, which he set near the rocky shoreline. The catch was kept in the well of the boat and brought back alive and kicking. After lighting the fire Dad filled the camp oven with water. Into this he placed the crayfish, and by the time the water boiled they were cooked. They scrabbled around a bit before succumbing and I thought this a rather cruel method of killing them, but Dad assured me it was the best way to do it. My slight trepidation regarding their dispatch didn't deter me from enjoying them.

Once they were ready a whole crayfish was deposited on your waiting plate to be eaten with salt and pepper and crusty bread. While the moon rose over the gum trees lighting up the sky we sat around the pit, cracking open the tail and legs and eating every tasty morsel before throwing the shells into the fire.

These were veritable feasts and certainly a luxury I can no longer afford.

When Dad's vacation of two weeks ended he had to go back home and go to work. The rest of us stayed at the shack and Dad returned on Friday nights. While he was away we weren't allowed to go fishing so we lived on corned beef, which seemed to last forever in the safe, plus tinned food. We ate spaghetti on toast, beans on toast and soup with toast. For dessert we had tinned peaches, apricots or pears liberally doused with Carnation milk. We also had an endless supply of Christmas puddings and delicious, buttery coconut cake.

When Dad returned on Friday nights we all raced to meet him and helped carry in the goodies he had brought. There was always warm crusty bread from the Sorell bakery. For tea we would have this bread slathered with melting butter and jam and a mug of tea made with fresh milk.

After Mum put the smaller children to bed us older ones kept an eye on them while Mum and Dad went for a walk along the beach. They always returned from these walks hand in hand looking happy, and we kids would know that all was right in our world.

For most of the time we had our shack and the world surrounding it to ourselves, but occasionally we had visitors.

Des and Chris came down with Auntie Barb quite a few times. She adored her little nephews and I think spent more time caring for them than Auntie Ron did.

It was on one of these holidays with our cousins that Chris pushed me out of the dinghy, nearly drowning me. On another I managed to alienate myself completely from Auntie Barb. Des lost a pocket knife that he had been given for Christmas and was very upset. She set us all to searching for it which we dutifully were doing until I noticed that Des was just sitting on the couch in the kitchen. I thought if he wasn't going to keep looking neither would I. When Auntie Barb saw I was no longer searching she demanded to know why, and I said because Des had stopped.

Suddenly she slapped me hard across the face saying, 'Don't you cheek me.'

I had never been hit by my parents and was stunned by her attack. My first reaction was to hit back which I did, landing a resounding slap on her cheek. The outcome of this altercation was a hurried departure of Barb and my cousins. Neither Dad nor Mum reprimanded me for this action, so either they thought it justified or were glad to see her leave, for she was an edgy presence around the place.

This altercation resulted in lifelong animosity between Barb and me, and even when I was an adult I found it difficult to be civil towards her.

Our other memorable visitor at the shack was Uncle Alf and one of his wives. We had never met him for he lived somewhere on the mainland, but he had come back for a visit. When I think back to the age I was at the time he must have come the summer after Grandma died, so he'd probably returned to collect his inheritance.

He looked nothing like our father, who was short and stocky with dark curly hair and lovely brown eyes. Alf was very tall with straight black hair and a fairly handsome face, spoilt by the fact that one of his eyes was slightly crossed. His wife, whose name I have forgotten, looked quite young and seemed very shy. They stayed with us at Tower Road for a while, then came down to the shack when we went on holidays. Dad and Alf seemed to get on okay. They went fishing during the day and played cards and drank beer together at night. I knew our Dad drank beer with his friends, but it was unusual for him to drink at home.

Mum didn't seem to mind the men drinking, but she was bothered by the way Alf's wife spent her time. She was quite a pretty woman with blonde hair down to her shoulders and very pale skin. We girls watched her with interest because she seemed to spend much of her day curling her hair, replenishing her lipstick or painting her nails. Having grown up with a mother who spent a minimum amount of time on personal adornment we were fascinated by this woman's beauty treatments.

Mum thought the poor woman wasted so much time on her grooming because she had nothing better to do. Our mother loved being outside and especially enjoyed swimming in the sea. Even when she was in her eighties she was always first into the water when we went to the beach. She was sure Alf's wife would enjoy herself more if she'd come outside and valiantly tried to get her out into the sun, to swim or walk the beach or wander up the hills amongst the trees. She couldn't understand how anyone would want to stay indoors when there were golden days out there to enjoy. Despite her efforts Mum failed to get the woman out of the shack, so in the end she left her with old copies of Readers' Digest and joined us on the beach.

After two weeks of this Dad left because he had to go to work during the week. Without his male companion Alf soon became bored. I think he'd also run out of cigarettes. Anyhow he said he was going to walk to Dunalley, a small village about five miles or eight kilometres from Connellys, and would buy fresh bread and milk there. He asked Mum if she needed anything else and was given a list with a few items Mum thought we might like. He set off with a cheerful wave, saying he'd be back by lunch time and would bring some extra goodies for us kids.

When he hadn't returned by late afternoon his wife became worried, but there wasn't anything she could do for we had no way of contacting him. When he hadn't returned by nightfall she was in tears. Mum tried to comfort her, but she was getting concerned as well. She said the next day she and we bigger kids would walk to Dunalley and see what had happened to him. We all went to bed rather worried about Uncle Alf and wondered where he could be.

The next day Mum was preparing to set off on the walk, taking Jane and me with her and leaving Shirl to help Alf's rather ineffectual wife look after the little kids. We thought it a bit of an adventure, and were disappointed when John raced up from the beach and said excitedly that Uncle Alf had just been dropped off by a fishing boat and was wading into the shore. We all ran down to the beach to welcome him home and help him with the shopping. He staggered ashore empty handed, a big boozy grin on his face. When his wife asked him where he'd been he went to put his arm around her shoulders and said cheerfully, 'Been with me mates. Give us a kiss Darling.' Then he lay down on the sand and went instantly to sleep, snoring loudly enough to frighten away the curious sea gulls.

His wife fled to the shack in tears, and Mum sent me up to the house to get a towel to cover his face so he wouldn't get sunburnt.

We went without the fresh bread and milk and other goodies he may have planned to acquire, but that didn't bother us. What did cause us concern was the frosty atmosphere in the house between Uncle Alf and his wife. Mum and Dad were always sort of peaceful together so we kids weren't used to grown-ups sniping at each other. We were all glad when Dad arrived on Friday night and some sort of harmony was restored. When Dad left on Sunday night Uncle Alf and his wife went with him and we weren't really sorry to see them go.

Before he left to return to the Mainland, Uncle Alf and Dad had an almighty blue. I don't know what it was about, but they began shouting at each other and finished up outside the house getting ready to have a fight. Dad was barely five foot seven and Alf towered over him at six foot one. I thought they looked a bit like the picture of David and Goliath that Miss Kippax had shown us in a book. We kids watched anxiously through the window while they squared off, then Dad landed a mighty punch on Alf's nose and he went screaming off down the street.

That was the last we ever saw of Uncle Alf. His name was never mentioned in our house, and we kids never found out what the fight was about.

A year or so later Dad came home with a newspaper called 'The Truth', and showed it to Mum. They read it together, and looked so upset about it Jane and I wondered what they were reading. Once they had put it in the garbage bin we retrieved it and took it into our bedroom. To our amazement there on the front page was a photo of Uncle Alf, looking decidedly the worse for wear. The headline read 'Hardly the Gay Lothario.' We weren't quite sure what was meant by the term 'Gay Lothario', but giggling rather nervously we read the text that followed. We gathered that our uncle was guilty of a crime called bigamy, something we had never heard of before. Evidently he had overlooked the small matter of obtaining a divorce from his wife in Tasmania before marrying first one woman and then another three. Altogether he had gone through a form of marriage with five women. Jane and I couldn't understand how he'd managed to talk so many women into marrying him because we thought him most unappealing.

For this crime of bigamy he served a prison sentence. I don't know how long he spent in jail for Mum and Dad never spoke of him, although they did go to his funeral some years later.

Even later a sixth wife, actually his second legal one, turned up in Tasmania with a son and Mum befriended her. She wasn't called Mrs Knight, but went under another name. Evidently Uncle Alf had changed his name after leaving prison, possibly to escape the notoriety his actions had brought him. I believe he met the woman who became his last wife when she nursed him through some illness in hospital. It seems he could still attract women, even when he was sick. This final wife was a quietly spoken rather conventional sort of woman, and I couldn't imagine her and Alf together, but perhaps he had settled down a bit in his later years.

Moving House

By the time of Uncle Alf's visit we were living in the house in Tower Road, for we had moved there earlier in the year.

When Nan died she left this house to Mum because she had bought it with money that had been left in trust to our mother by an old uncle. Mum didn't want to leave our home in Windsor Street but Dad was very keen to move. At the time I couldn't understand what Mum had against the move because the Tower Road house was bigger and nicer than the one we were in. When I was older I could totally understand why she felt this way. Not only had her mother died there only a few months earlier, but she was also displacing her sisters from the place that had been home to them for the previous decade.

Our parents had one of their rare disagreements about this proposed move, but in the end Dad got his way. We moved house in April, five months after Nan had died. She had left Barb and Ron a smaller house in North Hobart and they moved there with their husbands and Des and Chris. Later they sold this house and bought separate dwellings, so it must have proved too small for their continued co-habitation.

We girls absolutely loved the house in Tower Road for we were allocated the enormous upstairs bedroom with a dressing room off it. This was in fact the only bedroom in the house, which had originally been built for a wealthy bachelor and reflected his needs and tastes.

It had a large kitchen that you entered through the back door. Next to this was a spacious dining room, and both the kitchen and the dining room led to a long living room. This room had the staircase on one side and a door leading to an outdoor entertaining area that was roofed over by the bedroom above. To the left of the living room was another big room which led to a small sunroom at the front of the house. At the back of this room was the bathroom and laundry.

Although I'd often been to the house in Tower Road when Nan and the others were living there I hadn't taken any notice of how they utilised the spaces. I know Nan spent her days in the little sunroom, for that was where I sat with her when I visited, but whether she slept there as well I don't know. I think she must have.

Anyhow, it was not an ideal house for a large family and throughout the years there were various permutations of how the spaces were utilised. Initially we girls had the upstairs bedroom, Dad and Mum had the large side room as their bedroom. Bernard was only four months old so of course slept in the bassinet in the same room and John and Roger slept in the little sunroom off this. This worked all right while the boys were young, but Mum didn't like having them traipse through her bedroom to get to theirs when they were older. Peter, who became my first husband, earned her undying love when he was just a lad of eighteen by building a wall between the two rooms. From then on the boys went through the porch area to get to their bedroom and Mum had her much wanted privacy.

Jane and I thought our new home quite wonderful. Coming from a house where the main living room had been the kitchen to this place, that had two living rooms as well as the great semi-outdoor area, was a luxury. We still ate in the kitchen so the dining room became the one where we listened to the radio. The long lounge was where we sat to do our homework or play cards or curled up in front of the fire with a book, and the outside porch became a popular place to hang out with our 'gang' once we befriended the girls of our age who lived in the neighbourhood.

Throughout all the upheaval of packing up one house and moving to a new one with six children and a four-month old baby Mum was calm and outwardly cheerful. I only learnt much later how she hated that move and the reasons why. The only thing she actually complained about at the time was having to change from a fuel stove to an electric one, and it did seem to take a while before her scones were quite as light as they had been.

We had only been at Tower Road a short while when Grandma came to live with us. The smaller living room was made over into a bedroom for her, and from there she ruled the roost. She decided we girls didn't do enough to help our mother around the house, which was quite true, and from the time she took up residence she insisted that we clean and tidy a room each. We had previously helped with the washing up but often on an ad hoc basis. Grandma drew up a roster and made sure we stuck to it. We were also expected to help our mother with meals by peeling potatoes and scraping carrots. It was quite reasonable that we should help with these chores, but Mum had never demanded it of us so at times we grumbled amongst ourselves about how hard Grandma was.

We knew she was staying with us because she wasn't well, but she seemed quite spry and certainly had plenty to say about how we should behave. It was therefore a shock when she was taken to hospital and died of kidney failure. At the time it was said that she had 'rotten kidneys'. That she had polycystic kidneys was not diagnosed as the medical profession didn't seem to know much about it at that time, but the gene for this horrible disease has been passed down from her through the family with dire results. Dad died at seventy-five of kidney failure, and five of my sibling inherited the gene, which has been a contributing factor in the deaths of first Roger, then John, and a few years later my beloved Shirley. My youngest sister Val died recently. Although her husband gave her one of his kidneys the resulting discomfort she experienced from the crowding of three kidneys into a small space masked a further health problem.

Because I'd spent most of my young life in awe of Grandma and had never loved her the way I had my Nan, I didn't feel unduly upset when she died. This may sound horrible and heartless but that's how I felt. The thing that really upset me was when my Dad came into the house after the funeral and cried in Mum's arms. I had never seen our father cry, in fact I didn't think men cried, and he had always seemed the strongest of men. When I saw Dad in tears I went upstairs, lay on my bed and cried and cried. I thought that if he missed her so much she must have been nicer than she'd seemed to me, and now I would never get to love her.

Both of our parents had lost their mothers within the space of a year, but our house couldn't remain one of mourning for long. I guess with such a big and boisterous family to care for they felt they had to put their grieving aside and get on with life. Soon enough we girls reverted to our slack ways and no longer did a room each, but we did continue the washing up roster. I had also found I quite liked helping with the cooking so continued to do so.

I suppose the room where Grandma had slept must have been used by Alf and his wife when they stayed with us, but after the altercation it once more became a living room. Dad bought an enormous radiogram and Mum a new three piece lounge suite in autumn tones, and soon the room lost its imprint as a sickroom.

All the walls in the house were made of timber panelling and most were stained a dark brown. The only exceptions were the kitchen, bathroom, laundry and our bedroom. Mum said we girls could decorate our room however we wanted to. For some reason we decided we wanted a green and lilac room and we chose a strange shade of green, I think it's called eau de nil, and a pale, rather washed-out shade of lilac. When my tastes had matured somewhat I found this colour combination very sickly and quite appalling, but at the time we loved it and splashed paint around enthusiastically. We even painted a table and chairs that were on one side of the room and the timber dressing table. Mum bought green and lilac chintz fabric and made a skirt for this piece of furniture.

We thought the whole room looked absolutely lovely and glamorous and proudly showed it off to our new friends. Later, when we entered our teenage years, we all gathered in this room to try out new makeup and hair styles and plan what we would wear to dancing class or the Jazz House.

The Gang

The houses in Tower Road were all larger than the majority of those in Windsor Street, and most of the people who lived there were older retirees. We heard after we'd settled in that many of the residents hadn't been happy at the thought of a family with such a large number of children moving into their peaceful neighbourhood. Perhaps they'd thought we'd run wild in the street.

After the move John and Roger changed to a closer school but Jane and I continued to attend Moonah School, riding our bikes along the back roads. For a while I also rode out to Windsor Street on some weekends to visit Jack and Pat. During that year a massive building project had commenced in the top paddock above Windsor Street. Roads had been put through and houses were dotting up all over the empty expanses where we had played. When I visited we three still headed up to the paddock but now we wandered around building sites and climbed through partly built houses.

The last time I went to see them Jack wasn't home. I think he'd gone to the football with his father and I remember feeling a bit miffed at him for not being there. After talking to their mother for a while Pat and I headed up to the paddock. We had climbed across the framework of a partially built house and were gazing out what would be a window when a man appeared. He walked across the floor joists and joined us saying, 'Lovely view isn't it.' I didn't like the look of him much but answered politely that yes it was lovely. He moved closer and then said, 'Which of you girls has the biggest whistle.' I'd never heard this term before but I sensed that he was referring to our vaginas, or fannies as we called them. I moved quickly across the joists towards the doorway. Pat continued to stand near the window frame and the man put his arm around her shoulders. My heart was thumping and I said anxiously, 'Come on Pat.' She continued to stand there, the nasty man drawing her closer. She didn't seem to understand what he had asked or realise she was in some kind of danger. I did, but was too scared to go back for her for fear he'd grab me too. Even though I knew her father wasn't home I said in my sternest voice, 'If you don't come at once I'm going to get your father.' To my relief the man removed his arm and she scuttled across to me. I grabbed her hand and we ran all the way back to her place.

I think we told her mother about what had happened but I'm not sure. We may not have because of her bad nerves. I do know this was the last time I returned to my old street. So many of the places where we'd played were being altered beyond recognition and this incident somehow besmirched my happy memories.

I didn't see Jack again until several years later when I was sixteen and working as a junior teacher at Glenorchy School. We happened to meet when I was waiting for the tram and he was riding home from work on his bike. After that first meeting he was there every day and we'd talk until my tram arrived. The fondness we'd always had for each other was still there, and seeing him there each day rather reminded me of how he had waited for me after school during the time I was being harassed by Robert and Dennis. I know he wanted to build on this but I was going steady with Peter, the boy I later married, so I didn't encourage him. Despite this he dropped in at Tower Road one Saturday afternoon but Peter was there and seeing the two of us together must have made him realise nothing could come of our renewed friendship. After that visit he no longer waited each day at the tram stop and I never saw him again.

My final visit to Windsor Street had marked for me a transition from childhood to my teen years. Meeting Jack later after so many years was strange and made me realise how strong childhood bonds can be, but also how you can't go back.

With the move to Tower Road I had moved away from that life and those friendships, and Jane and I gradually befriended girls living nearby. In a short time we had formed our gang, and for the next few years the important part of our lives revolved around the times we spent together.

There were six of us, aged between eleven and thirteen, and when not at school we were inseparable. I was the youngest at eleven and Margie the oldest at thirteen and Di, Phil, Lesla and Jane ranged in age between us. Di and Lesla both had big, grown-up brothers and aging parents, Phil was the oldest in a family of five and Margie had brothers who were much younger than she. Her parents seemed quite young and were very welcoming if we gang members turned up, but their house was tiny. Phil's mum was a dear but her father was rather a gruff sort of man so we didn't go to her place much. Neither Lesla's nor Di's aging parents wanted to be inundated with a mob of girls.

Mum had always welcomed our friends and this larger house had plenty of room to accommodate six giggling and noisy girls, so our place became the gang's headquarters. The covered porch area and our spacious bedroom were both ideal places to hang out. In time we also created a cubby house under the roof. There was quite a large area under the sloping roof that you reached by going through our dressing room. We furnished this space with a small table and cushions, stuck drawings up on the walls and had a candle for illumination. We would go there to discuss secret plans and later to smoke cigarettes filched from Phil's father. Fortunately Dad caught us smoking before we set the house on fire and banned us from having matches up there. It didn't have the same atmosphere by torchlight as it previously had by candle light so we used it less after that.

At the time we formed our gang jeans were just becoming the in garment to possess. I had a beautiful light blue pair and Mum made me a white, blue and pink plaid shirt to go with them. Soon the whole gang was wearing jeans with the exception of Lesla whose mother thought them totally unsuitable attire for young ladies. Poor Lesla had to be content with wearing jodhpurs, which passed muster, according to her mother because young ladies in England wore them for horse riding. We all felt sorry for her for they were very daggy compared with jeans.

With the formation of our 'gang' I guess the worst fears of our elderly neighbour were realised, for now we moved as a group. We spoke together in our version of Pig Latin, in which you take the first letter of a word, put it on the end and add 'ay'. So 'What are we doing today?' became, 'Otway areay eeway oingday oodaytay.' When we spoke this gobbledygook we thought ourselves very smart and must have totally annoyed our parents and siblings with our chat, but this was half the fun.

We were all keen on the latest popular music, and every Saturday the gang gathered at our place to listen to the Hit Parade. The top ten most popular tunes of the week were played in reverse order, and we'd bet amongst ourselves about which would be the top tune of the week. We swooned to Eddie Fisher and Guy Mitchell, sang along with Frankie Lane, and of course went wild when we first heard Johnny Ray sing "Cry".

When the programme finished we often walked to Moonah, a nearby suburb where there was a shopping centre. All of the shops were closed on a Saturday except for the milk bar, which was always open. There we bought green spiders or chocolate milkshakes and occasionally lashed out on banana sundaes.

This milk bar was like an oasis of light in a sea of darkened shops, and it drew the young people who lived nearby like moths to a flame. Sometimes gangs of boys were also hanging out there and we exchanged chitchat with them, but we weren't interested in any of them romantically. At that time our shared friendship was pretty exclusive and we enjoyed being just us together.

We didn't always go straight home from the milk bar, but went wandering further afield. One night we went into the grounds of a church and fooled around frightening each other, making ghostly moaning noises and jumping out from the shadows. Another night we went into the grounds of Ogilvie High. You weren't meant to go there out of school hours, and we felt quite daring ignoring this ban. We ran around the building, found an open window and stole some stale biscuits from the home arts room and finished up spinning wildly like whirling dervishes in the middle of the oval under a grinning, golden moon.

On Sunday nights we listened to the Inner Sanctum Mysteries. These were frightening stories, so of course we deliberately heightened our fear by sitting crouched around the radiogram in our lounge room with the lights out. The programme always began with the sound of a creaking door and a spooky voice welcoming us to the inner sanctum. I don't remember any of the stories, but I know they were always scary and told with a maximum amount of melodrama.

By the time the programme finished we were all frightened and no-one wanted to go home alone. Phil and Margie lived the furthest away so Jane and I would walk as far as their houses with them and then race back home as quickly as we could.

We spent every weekend together, and many of the elderly people living in our streets frowned at us from their porches or gardens as we passed because we were so boisterous and noisy.

The exceptions were the old ladies who lived in a large house on the corner of Tower Road and Mercer Street, the street where Lesla and Phil lived. This house was called a rest home, but this was just a euphemism for a home for the aged. Previously I hadn't known such places existed, and I don't think there were many then, for most families still looked after their aged relatives until they died. The old ladies who lived there seemed reasonably spry, and were often to be seen sitting out on the wide verandah that ran across the front of the house. They knitted, crocheted and chatted to each other and appeared quite cheerful. When we passed they always smiled and waved at us and we waved back, for we felt that they at least approved of us. Perhaps we reminded them of grandchildren they no longer saw.

We heard via the grapevine that many of the other old ladies living in the area considered us unsuitably dressed when we wandered around together in our jeans and shirts. 'Aping men' was the term we heard used to describe us.

At that time we were attending Church Fellowship on Friday nights and the curate asked if any of us would take part in the concert being run by the church. Jane, Phil and I volunteered to sing and our offer was warmly received. We selected the songs carefully and practised our chosen numbers. On the night of the concert we wore our jeans and plaid shirts and added cowboy hats to our outfits. We swaggered onto the stage, indeed aping men, and sang an old country and western song, 'Cool, Clear Water,' and a new one made popular by Frankie Lane, 'Ghost Riders in the Sky'.

We received rousing applause and left the stage feeling we'd shown the old biddies we didn't care what they said about us.

During that first year as a gang we also befriended some of the boys in the area. Near the end of Tower Road was an empty paddock and the boys began building a bonfire there in preparation for Empire Night. This event was widely celebrated throughout the country for at this time, which was 1949, most Australians were still proud to be part of the British Empire. Many people of my parents and grandparents generations still referred to England as 'back home' even if they had never set foot on that small island on the other side of the world. 'God save the King' was played at all public events, and we even all stood while it was played before the first film at the picture theatres.

By the time I was sixteen I had become an ardent republican and refused to stand, much to the embarrassment of any boy who had been foolish enough to take me to the pictures. I think I was also one of the few people who didn't bother to go and see Queen Elizabeth when she visited Hobart in 1954.

In 1949 however I was still going along with the general sentiment of the country, and so our gang joined the local boys in building the bonfire to celebrate this night. We hunted up scraps of timber as well as old tyres donated by our fathers. By the time the night arrived we had an enormous pile and all of us had crackers of one kind or another. We girls favoured the pretty ones like Roman candles or flower pots but the boys had bangers and jack jumpers. Apart from one boy throwing a cracker at me that left tiny black specks in the back of one of my legs for a long time it was a very successful evening.

From that time we sometimes joined the boys in the paddock when they were playing football. I think they only let us join in because it gave them a reason to tackle us, but I didn't care about that for I loved having a chance to kick a ball. Growing up with a father who had been a good footballer and then an umpire, Jane and I had sometimes wished we could be boys so we could play this fabulous game. It pleases me that now many girls play soccer while at primary school and we also have girls' teams playing Australian Rules football.

Two of the boys we played football with lived in a large stone house next to the paddock, and this house was surrounded by the most amazing gardens. Now that we knew these boys they let us play in the gardens they called the Jungle.

At one time it must have been an orderly place of flowers and shrubs and fruit trees, but that time was long past. The whole property was earmarked for development and the boys' parents were renting the house while planning was under way. There were six boys in the family of varying ages. I don't think they were very well off for the boys all wore rather raggedy clothes, but I thought them so lucky to live where they did.

After years of neglect what must have once been magnificent ordered gardens had disappeared under long grass and various climbers and creepers that wound themselves around the trees. It was an absolute wonderland where orange and lemon trees still bore fruit amidst a tangle of ivy. I had never seen grapes growing before and didn't even know what a fig was, but here they survived and bore fruit in an environment of utter neglect and chaos.

Of course we picked any fruit we found and feasted on it in the various cubbies we made for ourselves amongst the trees. Sometimes we formed tribes and hunted each other through the jungle. Occasionally the boys took one of us prisoner and we would have to free our friend without being seen, but most of the time we just wandered around enjoying the place.

We lost this playground the following year when the boys and the rest of their family had to leave, and work began on a hostel for nurses. Later the Jungle was removed to make way for a housing settlement for English migrants.

Although we had lost this magic place Jane and I still had Connellys in which to run free. Naturally we had told the rest of the gang about our shack and of how wonderful the beach, the water and the surrounding hills were. We all decided it would be fun to go and stay there without parents or younger siblings. Of course none of our parents would agree to this, and said we were too young to look after ourselves. After much wheedling and whining they agreed to it as long as we had a responsible adult to look after us.

Jane and I talked Auntie Ron into accepting this responsibility and the rest of the gang were enthusiastic for they had met her and knew what a fun person she was. They liked that she wore bright clothes, colourful jewellery and lashings of makeup. On one occasion when she was visiting she gave us all a lesson in how to do the dance the Charleston and told us about what it had been like growing up as a flapper in the twenties. She was the ideal person to have as a chaperone.

Somehow we all crammed into her car along with quantities of food and clothes and chugged our way to the shack. We managed to manoeuvre our way across the marshland and were soon settled in and unpacked. Then we proudly led our friends down to the beach. The water was golden-green near the shore then merged from brilliant aqua to dark blue at the horizon, and the sand gleamed whitely in the sunlight. Our friends thought it quite as beautiful as we had described.

We spent a joyous week there, glorying in the sense of freedom we felt from being away from home and family, with only a kindred and understanding adult to supervise us.

We swam and sun baked or walked the beach with long, twining bunches of kelp tied around our waists and iridescent mermaids necklaces around our necks. We pretended we were island princesses or glamorous film stars. I still opted to be Betty Grable but now Jane was Dorothy Lamour. We sashayed along the hot silvery sand singing at the top of our voices, 'Sing Me a Song of the Islands' and 'Some Enchanted Evening'. Perhaps we imagined an exciting stranger might appear, but we really didn't want one to, for we felt brilliantly detached from the rest of the world.

Most evenings we crowded around the big open fire and cooked crumpets that we ate dripping with butter and crimson homemade jam, or toast topped with spaghetti or baked beans. One night we lit a fire on the beach and cooked potatoes in the ashes and bacon on sticks. Another night we took Dad's spear and punt and tried our luck at catching flounder, but we were so noisy I think we frightened the fish away.

Auntie Ron proved to be the accommodating chaperone we had hoped for. She didn't care unduly about us getting a balanced diet or worry about when we ate or where we wandered, but sat peacefully in the sun and read.

On the last night we decided we wanted to sleep outside. Auntie Ron said she didn't think it was a good idea for she thought it was going to rain, but we talked her into letting us. We dragged and carried the heavy iron beds outside, ignoring a hairy grey tarantula that scuttled across the sandy floorboards. As we set up our beds in various places under the gum trees we laughed and joked about whose house was best. We were girls on the cusp of womanhood, acting out what would become reality in a few short years.

The night was warm and starlit, but suddenly the sky darkened and lightening flashed across the distant hills. In an urgent flurry we bundled our bedding together and fled indoors, leaving the beds to be pelted by hard rain. Ron laughed at us but refrained from saying, 'I told you so,' as we settled down with our mattresses on the floor and the rain pounded loudly on the tin roof.

The next day was bright and sunny as we dragged the beds back inside and tidied up before all cramming back into Auntie Ron's car for the trip home. It had been a fabulous holiday and chance for us to have a little bit of independence.

The Gang Goes Out

Our holiday at the shack took place at the beginning of 1950. This was a momentous year for me for I started high school, learnt to deal with a stalker on my own and went on dates with my first real boyfriend.

None of the other gang members attended Hobart High. Shirley did, but she was four years ahead of me and in her matriculation year. At this time we weren't particularly close and she often played sport or hung around with friends after school. As a result I walked home by myself after getting off the trolley bus at New Town Station.

If the stationmaster wasn't watching I walked along the railway line until I reached the bridge that went over the track at Tower Road. If I was unable to take this shorter route I walked down the road next to the line, along Risdon Road and up Swanston Street. An alternative route was up Cut-throat Alley. This was a very steep, narrow lane, bounded on one side by a paling fence and on the other by a high bank on top of which was the train line. The alley began at Risdon Road and ended up in a short street that joined Tower Road.

I often varied which way I went from choice, but after the stalker appeared on the scene I went wherever he wasn't.

My first encounter with him occurred as I was just about to enter Cut-throat Alley. I'd noticed a man standing under the train line bridge that went over Risdon Road but hadn't thought anything of it. I had just started walking along the level part of the alley when he came up behind me, grabbed me by the shoulders and said, 'I'm gunna have you.'

I saw his yellow teeth grinning at me and felt him pushing me further into the alley. I pulled free of his clutching hands and ran like mad, too frightened to even look back to see if he was following.

From that day he would be waiting, sometimes at the station, and at other times under the bridge or further along the road. If I saw him I would run as fast as I could in the opposite direction. Getting home from school became a nightmare. Each day I looked anxiously out the bus window as it pulled into the stop to see if I could see where he was, and planned my route in advance. It reminded me of how I'd felt when eluding Robert and Dennis, but now I was on my own. Strangely I didn't tell Mum about my problem or either of my older sisters, and I don't know why not.

It all finally came to an end very simply. One day I didn't see him anywhere around as I walked down to Risdon Road, so I thought it was safe to take the shorter route up Cut-throat Ally. I was halfway up when I saw him coming behind me. I sped up but could hear him getting closer and closer and was terrified. Suddenly he grabbed hold of me around my waist. Because the alley was so steep his head was level with my arm, and I swung my brief case as hard as I could. It connected to his head with a satisfying thump. He gave a yelp, let go of me and I raced away.

That was our final encounter for from then on he stopped stalking me, and while it was traumatic at the time the outcome gave me confidence that I could look after myself.

As I've said I was the only one in the gang going to Hobart High. The rest of the girls all went to Ogilvie except for Margie and she attended Moonah Modern School. A school friend of Margie's was having a birthday party and told her she could invite us along. It was there that I met Frank.

The birthday girl lived out beyond the final tram stop in Glenorchy so we walked from there to her house. It was a rather old rambling sort of house sitting in the middle of a large paddock. There were lots of boys and girls at the party, but we didn't know any of them so sort of stuck together. After we had eaten the usual party food and sung happy birthday we all went outside to play games.

By then it was getting dark, and the birthday girl decided we would play catch a girl kiss a girl. I had kissed the odd boy or two during minor crushes at primary school and Jack and I had exchanged the occasional peck, but these were big boys of fourteen and fifteen. I was grabbed by one and kissed rather sloppily and lingeringly. As I was escaping from him I saw a particularly ugly boy advancing towards me. I ran and hid behind a tree and I'm ashamed to say burst into tears. I'd thought I was old enough to be at a teenage party, but I wasn't enjoying this game that seemed to have the other girls screaming with delight. As I sat there on a log feeling miserable a rather nice-looking boy I had noticed earlier came and sat beside me and asked what was wrong. I told him that I didn't like being kissed by just anyone, and he said he'd stay and look after me. We exchanged names and he put his arm around me protectively. We chatted companionably while the hurly burly of catching and kissing continued around us.

When the party ended he walked with me and the gang to the tram stop, but we had missed the last tram home so had to walk.

It was a lovely warm night and I walked home with his arm around my waist while the rest of the gang and

Frank's brother David ambled along behind or in front of us. When we reached home Frank asked if he could kiss me goodnight and I had my first grownup kiss that I enjoyed.

Thus began my first experience of dating. Frank was sixteen and already working and I was a twelve and a half year-old school girl.

For the next few months I met Frank outside the Moonah Picture Theatre every Saturday night. He paid for our tickets and we sat together holding hands during the first film. At interval he always bought a box of chocolates, most of which I ate for he seemed diffident about taking any. During the second half he would put his arm around my shoulders and we exchanged the odd chocolaty kiss. Afterwards he walked me home and came in to the house for tea and biscuits provided by Mum, then we kissed goodnight at the front gate before he left to walk home.

On Sundays the gang always hung out at our place, and now Frank and his brother David joined us. I'd make cheese straws and Mum always had kiss biscuits or rock cakes in the tins. We'd sit around in the covered verandah, drinking tea, eating and talking. We had a very old windup gramophone and only two records that we tried to dance to. Unless someone kept winding the music slowed and we found it hilariously funny trying to dance to it. We took exaggeratedly long steps as we slow danced, and then jigged in time as someone wound it up again.

Later in the afternoon Frank and I would slip away from the group for a quiet kiss in the back yard before he and David jumped the fence and walked along the rough path above the train line to Moonah where they lived.

Our little romance came to an abrupt and very unsatisfactory end. One Sunday John and Roger lay in wait for Frank and David and pelted them with stones as they were walking along the path on their way home. I don't know why my brothers did this or why I didn't try to stop them, but I didn't. In fact I thought Frank and David rather cowardly to run away the way they did. In retrospect I realise there was nothing else they could have done, but at the time I was just embarrassed by the incident. The following Saturday the gang and I went to the pictures as usual, but I turned away when I saw Frank waiting for me and went into the theatre with the girls. It's possible he thought I had encouraged my brothers' behaviour for from that time we didn't speak.

Soon our gang began to spread our wings and find other forms of entertainment than the pictures so I didn't see Frank again. I was left with the rather uncomfortable feeling that I had treated him badly by not apologising for the way in which my brothers had behaved and for dropping him without an explanation.

That summer on Sundays we girls usually caught the double-decker tram down to Sandy Bay beach. We'd sit on the top level, and as it swayed around the bends and rattled along the straight we'd sing songs like 'Irene Goodnight' and 'On Top of Old Smokey' at the top of our voices. We were young, brash and exhibitionistic.

Once we arrived at the beach we headed for the lawn that ran down to the sand. After settling ourselves on our towels we'd proceed to flirt with nearby groups of boys, swim out to the punt that was moored in the bay, eat ice creams and chips and generally have fun. When autumn arrived and swimming and sunbathing days came to an end for the year we once more spent Sunday afternoons on the covered verandah. By this time we had taken up skating and were now joined by various boyfriends we had met at the rink.

The huge outdoor skating rink was built not far from where we lived and was said to be the biggest outdoor rink in the Southern Hemisphere. We were soon spending every Friday and Saturday night there. Initially we had to queue to hire the black skating boots, many of which were old with blunt blades. After we had learnt to skate we nagged our parents into buying us white skating boots and proper clothes. Mum made me a little gingham dress with a full swirling skirt and a short blue pleated skirt that I wore with a cream jumper with Fair Isle patterning on the yoke. This jumper was pure wool and handmade and frightfully expensive, but somehow I talked Mum into buying it for me for my fourteenth birthday. From memory I think it cost five pounds which was quite a lot of money in those days.

The year I turned fourteen our gang's obsession with skating almost ruled our lives. From our homes we could hear the music coming from the rink, and it acted like a magnet to draw us there in much the same way that music at a show or regatta draws people in. Each night we'd rush through our homework, or simply pretend to do it, because then we would be free to go skating. Once we had our own skates, and no longer needed an entrance ticket to hire the hideous black ones, we began sneaking into the rink during the week. We'd walk along the path above the railway line, climb through a fence then amble nonchalantly to the grandstand where we'd put on our skates. We'd then take to the ice, gliding gracefully alone or in pairs or skating furiously during the speed skating sessions.

We didn't feel particularly guilty about sneaking in like this because we knew we would only be there for about an hour, and we always paid on Friday and Saturday nights.

Besides skating, boys had also become an important part of our lives, and there were always new ones turning up at the rink. We skated with them and allowed them to buy us coffee when we warmed up before the huge open fire. Sometimes we let them walk us home, and kissed them goodnight with promises of further meetings at the rink, but if a handsomer boy took our fancy we ignored the boy from the previous night. One boy who I dated for about four weeks wouldn't accept the fact that I was no longer interested in him, and sat outside our house on his motorbike every night for weeks after we'd broken up. Another sat on the bridge that crossed Tower Road and waited to see me when I came home from school. Although I wouldn't even stop and talk he did this for some time. I felt guilty about both these boys but also annoyed, for I was a heartless little bitch.

As a group we were fascinated by boys, but we treated them with a fair degree of disdain. We flirted with them, allowed them to kiss us, but dropped or swapped them quite heartlessly. We didn't consider what it was like for them walking home late at night through deserted streets because they had missed the last tram, or how they felt when we kissed them one week and ignored them the next. For a brief time we were queen bees and made the most of it, for we sensed that we were destined to become worker bees like our mothers in the not too distant future.

Our hedonistic life began to take its toll on school results, and at the end of the year I barely scraped through and Jane failed and would have to repeat year nine or C class as it was called then. Mum and Dad were not happy with our reports and curtailed our social activities when school resumed. We were only allowed out Friday, Saturday and some Sunday nights.

It was at about this time that we met the 'Swiss Boys'. They were all brilliant skaters, having learnt in Switzerland as boys. We were enchanted with them for they were a handsome, laughing trio and strangely enough they found us equally attractive, although we were only school girls and they were grown men. Soon we had paired off, Phil with Bertie, Jane with Wally and me with Charlie, who at twenty-seven was the oldest and I thought by far the handsomest. He was tall and well-built and had the most beautiful aquiline nose, lovely grey eyes and chiselled lips. If this sounds like the description of a hero from a Mills and Boon novel I make no excuses, for this is how he looked, or at least how I remember him.

When I told my children about my brief love affair with Charlie they couldn't understand how their Nan and Granddad had let Jane and me go out with men who were so much older than we were. I suppose it was rather strange, but somehow the age differences didn't seem important, and I think this was because they were all very youthful in their ways. They gained the same sort of enjoyment from skating as we did and had about them an air of joie de vivre. They jointly owned and ran a small business making smallgoods, and sometimes after skating we would all go out to the factory while they did strange things to meat in bubbling cauldrons or packed sausages for the next day's delivery. They appeared to take their work as lightly as their play and fitted it in around enjoying life.

Jane turned sixteen while we were going with our 'Swiss Boys' and wanted to have a party at night to celebrate. Mum and Dad had met Charlie and Wally frequently because we always took our boyfriends in for cups of tea after an evening out. Our parents agreed to the party as long as there was no alcohol. When we told our boyfriends about this stipulation they said they were happy to go along with it.

On the night of the party Mum got the younger siblings to bed early and she and Dad retired to their room leaving us the run of the house. Charlie, Wally and Bertie turned up bearing quantities of soft drinks and a lovely present for the birthday girl. Nearly everyone was having a good time, eating the food Mum had prepared, dancing to music on the new radiogram and drinking soft drinks when our evil cousin Chris arrived. Di was feeling a bit left out because she didn't have a boyfriend at the time and Chris began paying her attention. We didn't notice what was going on until Di became violently ill, and we realised Chris had brought a bottle of rum or whiskey and had been plying her with drink. She was nearly paralytic.

Chris was ordered out of the house and Charlie and Wally offered to take Di home. She lived just up the street from us and they virtually had to carry her. When her mother opened the door and saw the state Di was in she roundly abused them for getting her daughter drunk. Despite their protestations she didn't believe them, and grabbed Di and slammed the door in their faces. The rest of us thought it most unfair that they were blamed for Chris's wrongdoing, but the boys didn't seem to mind.

During that year the boys organised an ice hockey team and there were a few matches between them and some teams from the mainland. The team used to practise after the rink closed for the night and we would watch them. We were allowed to skate on the empty rink once practice was finished. I'll never forget how free and happy I felt skating and twirling around that nearly empty rink either alone or hand in hand with Charlie.

Shortly after Jane's party I was sitting in the van with Charlie and he put his hand on my breast while we were kissing. I felt myself responding to his touch and really, really wanted him to leave his hand there, but knew it wouldn't be right. We were given a tremendous amount of freedom, but never left home without Mum's advice to 'behave like little ladies at all times'. I figured petting with Charlie didn't fit this criterion.

Despite the fact that I loved kissing him I knew I wasn't ready for a sexual relationship, and I didn't want him to consider me a tease, so asked him to remove his hand.

He said smiling down at me, 'What is the harm, my little girl.'

Feeling a bit flustered, I said, 'Well perhaps I am a little girl but it's my breast.'

He took his hand away and we kissed some more, but that incident made me start to think perhaps he was too old for me; that he should be with someone older who was ready for a more physical relationship.

The next time we were all at the skating rink I flirted with a younger boy and went home with him. That was the end of Charlie and me. Sometime later he began going with an older woman. She must have been all of nineteen and very attractive in a sleek, stylish way. Although I still thought him one of the handsomest men I'd ever seen, and felt a little pang of jealousy seeing him with another woman, I didn't regret letting him go. I was glad he'd found someone more suitable and approved his choice.

At about this time our absolute obsession with skating was beginning to wane and we began attending Mrs Ds. dancing classes which were held on Friday nights. These classes were where many of the town's teenagers went to learn to dance, and more importantly meet members of the opposite sex.

Before the dance we gang members met at our house to check our hairdos and admire each other's clothes, then caught the tram into town. We all wore very full skirts held out by stiff starched petticoats, pretty blouses and extra wide belts. Usually we carried a cardigan in case the night turned cold. Our skirts were so full and stiff we had trouble fitting next to each other on the narrow seats on the tram. We giggled about this, and sometimes older women looked at us critically because of our noise, but with the insolence of youth we ignored their prune-like faces.

When we arrived in town we'd get off the tram and walk the short distance to dancing class. It was held in a hall that had an entry foyer where you paid to go in. Off this foyer was a cloakroom where we left our cardigans before going inside. The room had a highly polished floor and a small raised stage at one end where the three piece band was set up.

If a dance was already in progress when we arrived we filed in sedately and sat on the chairs positioned around the edge of the room. When a bracket finished the boys escorted their partners back to their seats before returning to the boys' side of the room. During the break we'd look across at the boys and decide which boy we wanted to dance with. This was a sort of game we played and added to the fun; although it didn't always work out the way you wanted it to.

Mrs D. was a prim, middle-aged martinet and she insisted on correct dance room etiquette. If a boy asked you to dance you were duty bound to accept so we spent the intervals eyeing off the good-looking lads and avoiding eye contact with those who were less appealing.

When the next dance was announced there would be a scramble across the room, and it was a relief when the boy you had chosen stood before you asking for the pleasure of the next dance. While dancing you tried to make conversation, but you needed to concentrate on getting the steps right or Mrs D. or one of her assistants would intercept and correct you.

When the number finished the boy escorted you back to your seat. If you'd clicked he'd say quickly, 'Perhaps we can have another dance later.'

The evening continued with the quickstep, followed by a waltz, a schottische, the pride of Erin and the always-popular progressive barn dance. Before the new or more difficult dances Mrs D. and her partner gave a demonstration of the steps then some unlucky boy and girl were chosen to dance a further demonstration. We all breathed a sigh of relief when we weren't chosen because the dancing partner was a sleazy little man. It was said of him that he sometimes made a pest of himself with some of the girls unlucky enough to dance a demonstration with him.

One of the many regulations was that you weren't to dance with the same partner all the time. If a boy liked you he asked to have the last dance with you, which was an indication that he wanted to take you home. If you liked him you agreed, and would look forward to the tram trip and a cuddle in the street as he walked you home. If you really liked him you invited him in for a cup of tea and later a smooch on the couch. Conversely if he didn't appeal on closer inspection you would kiss briefly at the gate, and make a hypocritical agreement to see him the following week at dancing class.

Dancing gradually replaced skating as our favoured pastime and we began spending Saturday nights at the Jazz House. This was entirely different from dancing class and much more exciting. We spent most of Saturday deciding what to wear. By this time Shirl had qualified as a physical education teacher and returned home. She was teaching at Hobart High and earning good money, most of which she spent on clothes. I was fortunate enough to be the same size as Shirl, and she was very generous so I now had access to the wardrobe of a smart eighteen year-old.

The clothes we wore to the Jazz House differed from our dancing class dresses. Generally we wore tight skirts with fitted tops or sweaters or slightly more sophisticated outfits. Shirl had a particularly lovely dark green dress with a scoop neckline that I sometimes borrowed. With it I wore big gold hoop earrings and felt very sophisticated and glamorous in that outfit. I also had a lovely red skirt and matching top made out of a material called faille. Mum made this for me as well as a black top of the same material that I could also wear with the skirt. I wore these outfits with a wide black belt. They were quite grown-up clothes for a fifteen year-old but I think our dear mother enjoyed seeing me looking good in the clothes she made.

Once more we girls caught the tram into town, but we were quieter and behaved more maturely than we did on Friday nights. We felt we should behave in a more grown-up way because we were going to the Jazz House, and this was a place that wasn't only for kids but attracted older people in their twenties and thirties. It was also a popular meeting place for the bodgies and widgies who were the fringe group around town. They fascinated us with their unusual clothes and haircuts and the way they seemed to thumb their noses at normal society.

The Tom Pickering band that played there was considered to be the second best in Australia at the time, not far behind the famous Graeme Bell Jazz Band. We considered ourselves very lucky to have them.

As we got off the tram we'd hear the sound of a favourite New Orleans blues number throbbing in the night air, and it became louder as we climbed the narrow staircase leading to the dance hall. It felt as though the music was drawing us into a place of excitement and fun.

We paid at the door and left our coats in the cloakroom. Unless we arrived during a break we entered into a darkened room where only the stage was dimly lit. Often we arrived as the clarinettist was playing a solo bracket and we'd stand transfixed as he improvised around the melody, going higher and higher then finishing on a long pure note that sent a shiver down my spine. The rest of the band would join back in to complete the number while everyone clapped. There would be a feeling of camaraderie and warmth in the room that you get when a group of people share a great moment.

We always headed for the left hand side of the room for there was a sharp delineation of where one stood during the intervals. When the lights were turned back on we'd look across the room at the short-haired widgies in their black tight dresses and their boyfriend bodgies who all wore big-shouldered zoot suits in various bright colours. They enthralled us for they were the rebels around town, but you didn't dare look at them too closely or a widgie was likely to cross the floor and threaten to fight you. Their presence added a sense of danger and wilfulness to the evening.

Usually the bodgies and widgies danced together. They were always the first on the floor and knew the latest steps, which they performed very showily. Occasionally a bodgie sauntered across the floor and asked a 'good girl' for a dance, but the widgies were definitely out of bounds for the straight guys.

With the exception of this unwritten rule there were no regulations as those that abounded at dancing class. If you liked someone you could dance together all night, but generally it was more fun to dance with several different boys. If a boy wanted to take you home he always asked well before the end of the evening, and you always had the last dance together.

The tram trip home would be much the same as after dancing class. Sometimes you found a boy easy to talk to and fun to be with, but other times you'd discover that someone who had seemed exciting on the darkened dance floor was quite boring on the hard seat of a brightly lit tram. If this was the case you fobbed him off with a brief kiss at the gate, but if the boy appealed on closer inspection you invited him in for a cup of tea and a chance to get to know him better.

Many years later when I watched a programme on television about speed dating it reminded me of the dating methods of my youth. We met a lot of boys, assessed them after a brief meeting and spent more time with those we found appealing.

Often the decade in which I reached my teens is referred to as the boring fifties, but for me it was a great time to be young and not at all boring. We were the first generation to wear jeans and dress in a distinctively different way from our parents. We were also the first group to have divergent tastes in music from those of our parents. Most of them couldn't stand Johnny Ray and didn't appreciate the driving sounds of Bill Haley and his Comets. The fifties was also the decade when Elvis Presley appeared on the scene and shocked the oldies with the way he moved once he began to appear in films.

I remember being blown away the first time I heard 'Heartbreak Hotel'. You didn't have to see him to know here was a man who could make you believe he felt what he sang. Actually Dad, who was quite musical and had a nice baritone voice, thought Elvis could sing, but he said the only reason Johnny Ray could stand his own caterwauling was because he was deaf.

During the fifties dancing changed totally as we moved away from the conventional ballroom dances to jive, rock and roll and later the twist. These led to many variations, and eventually to the stage where it is now considered all right to dance alone.

It was the first decade when teenagers were seen as a separate group, a sub-species some might say, instead of children or young adults.

There were no major wars being waged and it was relatively safe for girls to go where they wished without the fear of being mugged. Of course there were always dubious characters around and I think I met my fair share of them, but they were easily deterred. Attacks of women and children seem to be more prevalent and more violent now.

The legal drinking age was twenty-one so there was very little drinking done by teenagers. There weren't any drugs around except for cigarettes, and at that time they were considered cool for practically all the film stars smoked on screen.

The fear of pregnancy kept most of us on the straight and narrow, and when a girl succumbed it was generally with a steady boyfriend. There were certainly plenty of rushed marriages, but sexually transmitted diseases were a rarity. So although we ranged free it was in a world of relative safety.

The Gang Moves On

By the beginning of 1953 I was the only gang member still at school. Jane left shortly after turning sixteen in June 1952 and Phil, Lesla and Di completed B class at the end of that year. The following year I completed B class year and obtained a reasonably good Schools Board Certificate but had never really taken these important years of study seriously. There had been so much going on in my social life that school had been of secondary importance. I also didn't make close school friendships because the girls in our gang were my main friends.

The year after leaving school I was employed as a junior teacher and the following year completed the one year teacher training course at Launceston Teacher's College. This was the minimum qualification at that time in order to become a teacher.

In later years I came to regret my lack of education so returned to my old high school that was now Hobart Matriculation College. I matriculated from there at the ripe old age of thirty-seven and then went to university. This was not something I would even have envisioned doing back then in the early fifties because I was heartily sick of being a school girl and felt ready to begin life as an adult.

At about the time three of us were going with the Swiss Boys we had lost touch with Margie when she started going steady with a boy we actually never met. We were rather shocked to hear that, at sixteen, she was pregnant and getting married. It was a very rushed affair and she didn't invite any of us to the wedding. About four years later I ran into her at the tram stop when I was doing my first year as a teacher at Glenorchy School. She was noticeably pregnant and had two small boys with her aged about two and three. She would have only been twenty but looked tired and worn and wore a drab grey coat that pulled tight over the bump. We said a brief hello and I boarded the tram. Watching her from the tram window as she walked away holding the hands of her two small boys I felt totally saddened by how she had changed. She had been such a pretty teenager but now looked like a drab housewife.

Phil was the next to wed. Shortly after Charlie and I broke up Wally returned to Switzerland, but Bertie and Phil continued to see each other. There wasn't quite the age gap between them that there had been between Charlie and I, for Bertie was only twenty-three when Phil was fifteen. They married when Phil was eighteen.

Jane met Eric, who was a bodgie, at the Jazz House and after an on again off again relationship they married when she was nineteen.

I also met my future husband at the Jazz House. Although he was still a school boy he had been drinking so I refused his pleas to dance with him and ignored him as I left the dance hall with another boy. We met the following week at dancing class where he was sober and apologetic about the way he had been the previous week. We danced together a couple of times and I agreed to let him escort me home. I found Pete very attractive and we spent a lot of time together, but I considered we were both too young to go steady. I continued to go out with other boys for a further year, but slowly realised I was happiest with Pete. We married when we were nineteen and twenty-one respectively. He actually never forgave me for continuing to date other boys after we met, and brought this up during arguments for many years after we married.

I think Lesla was about twenty-three when she married. In those days this was almost considered being on the shelf, but now it would be thought quite young. We went to her wedding, but lost touch with her soon after for she married a man in the air force and he was posted to the mainland.

I have no idea what happened to Di but I think she moved to the mainland.

In the section about our gang's holiday at the shack I wrote of how we laughingly joked about whose house amongst the gum trees was best, and that 'We were girls on the cusp of womanhood, acting out what would become a reality in a few short years'.

It was only while writing this that I realised what a very short time we were 'the gang', but it was a time of such fun and freedom; of experiencing different things and meeting many different boys; a time of living in the moment and making the most of each moment lived.

I wouldn't have missed it for quids.

Going Back

Once I began writing this memoir I was curious to know what the world in which I had lived so many years ago looked like now.

As mentioned earlier I returned to Moonah School and was so pleased to learn that Mr Truscott was to have a memorial plaque installed in his honour. I was also thrilled to see the tree I had planted still flourishing and to learn that the plaque was to be placed at the base of this tree.

Other things had changed beyond recognition. The class rooms around the quadrangle had been extended out so that what remains is much smaller and filled with plants in pots. It certainly looks much more cheerful and welcoming than the big shaded area where we had lined up before marching into school.

The playgrounds are also totally different. The wild and weed-filled area where I played as a girl now contains an orderly vegetable garden and next to it is a building where the produce from the garden is cooked and eaten. The pine trees from which we obtained the needles to protect us from the canings are gone. I was told most of them had blown down during a fierce storm some years earlier.

I next returned to Windsor Street and stopped outside the house where I spent my first ten years. The verandah, where Mum curled our hair while she told us the story of 'Lonely Betty', has been removed to make way for a large bow window in the front room. The house looks different but well cared for, but the biggest shock was the size of the back yard. It is now very small and old people's units snake around behind the house that was built next door and where Dad's garage used to be. The row of pine trees in which we had spent so many happy hours has been removed. Fortunately there are two trees, of the same variety as those in which we climbed, still growing near the fence of the big house opposite our old home. I could see that they were just as soft and spreading as I remembered.

I had known that the mansion at the bottom of the street had disappeared somehow beneath what had become Glen View, a home for the aged. I thought it had been pulled down to make way for newer buildings, and hadn't realised until I took a close look that it still remains surrounded by new structures. You can see the grey slate roof and at least four chimneys rearing up from the mishmash around them. The only traces left of the once magnificent gardens are two large trees that stand like sentinels either side of the entrance.

It was strange to see these places where we had played as children filled with units for old people. As I stopped to take a photo of the roofline of the mansion, an old white-haired lady trudged past on a walking frame. In my imagination I had been back in my childhood days, and as I watched her I felt a pang of loss for a time that was gone, and the shadow of what I suppose must eventually befall me.

I drove to the top of the street to see if anything up there looked familiar.

I knew the quarry had been filled in when a school was built on that piece of land and that the paddock and orchards where we had roamed free would no longer be there. The land slopes down and I imagined this was where we had ridden the sledge we had found beneath a briar bush. Nothing else was vaguely familiar for now those empty spaces are a maze of winding streets and closely packed houses.

I had an idea the avenue remained for I had glimpsed a gap between the Telecom building and a car park. I drove away from Windsor Street and parked on the main road near to where the avenue commenced. A cold wind was blowing and it scattered papers and other debris that lay on the ground surrounding a sign that read, 'Private Property' and underneath 'No Unauthorised Access'. Being basically law-abiding I didn't venture past the sign but I looked up the avenue hoping to see the lilacs and rosebushes and the golden chain and almond trees. All that remains are a few sickly-looking pine trees and unkempt grass.

I didn't need to revisit the Grove for I knew that the large grassy area, the change rooms and the long swing Jack and I often played on were long gone. This place is now home to the Derwent Entertainment Centre and the associated car park.

My next stops were at the places of my teenage years. Our old house in Tower Road is difficult to see from the road, for trees that were once small now encroach on the dwelling, hiding it from view and probably making it very dark inside. It has an air of neglect, with paint peeling off weatherboards and ivy creeping under the eaves.

I knew the skating rink, where our gang had spent so many joyous hours at the beginning of the 1950s, was long gone. Shortly after we began attending dances instead of the skating rink there were two separate fires there in the space of twelve months. This caused the closure of the rink in 1953. Rumours abounded that the fires had been deliberately lit by the owners to collect insurance. I don't think the rumours were true as the owners appear to have ended up owing the Tasmanian government quite a lot of money.

The Jungle, where we had spent such magical times, also disappeared in the early 50s. It had been uprooted to make way for housing but I wondered if some small vestige might remain. On closer inspection the old stone house still stands and looks in good condition, but it has had a very basic weatherboard extension tacked onto it. The barn that once overlooked the Jungle has been more sympathetically added to, and houses some commercial enterprise. There are now neat brick houses on tiny blocks where that once chaotic and exciting playground had flourished. Near the creek that marked the end of the Jungle a few remnant vines remain twining around shrubby bushes and diseased trees. I paused there for a moment remembering how beautiful and exciting the place had been.

Before leaving that area I drove down the short street where Cutthroat Alley emerged. It was gravel when I walked up it in my youth and is now bitumen. It looks even steeper than I remembered it, but I could see how this steepness had been to my advantage when I finally dealt with my stalker. It still seems quite a scary little track to me, although I know I walked it frequently after I had got rid of him.

The one place that has remained a constant in my life has been Connellys Marsh, and it is still as magical to me as it was when I first came here as a four year old. Of course there have been big changes throughout the last seventy-eight years.

Probably the biggest difference is that the marsh was drained when developers planned to build a small subdivision at that end of the beach. This project never materialised, but large blocks were sold off and there are some houses dotted around where once there were only ghostly gums and stunted shrubs trying to survive in the damp acidic soil.

The lagoon at the end of the beach, where we spent our first few summers, is smaller than it was for there has been a build-up of sand at the mouth of the stream that feeds into the sea. The beach itself seems to have developed a slope through the years and it doesn't look as flat to me as it was, but there are still the islands at low tide that we played on as children. The marram grass covered banks were seriously eroded one winter. This happened during a storm that combined with a king tide to eat them away, and we residents hope this is not the beginning of the effects of global warming.

Along the beach front there have been many changes since the days when Dad and Narna had the only shacks here. Now there are modern houses all along the beach front and only two or three of the older shacks remain

Our shack burnt down during a bushfire when I was seventeen and Dad then built a large tin structure on the beach where he'd previously had the small boatshed. He called this new building a boatshed but we used it as a shack for it had beds, a cooking area and later even a fridge.

John had a timber house moved to where the old shack had been and Bernard and I built brick beach houses next door. When Dad died he left the land to be shared equally between all of us, and now all my siblings or their kids have a place here.

This beautiful spot has been a joy and a solace to me throughout the years. I spent so much of my childhood here and also my teen years. Pete, my first husband, holidayed with us when he and I were teenagers. He loved it as much as I did, so we spent the second week of our honeymoon here. Once I had children I brought them to Connellys for holidays, and when my second marriage disintegrated this was where I came to heal and make a new life for myself. I enlarged my original dwelling, planted natives in the front and sides and built up the sandy soil to grow vegetables in the places that are sheltered from the sea winds.

Soon I had grandchildren who came to stay. They played on the sand, swam in the water and we played hide-and-seek around my native gardens. Sometimes they were here at the same time as their second cousins, and my remaining siblings and I watched dotingly as these precious grandchildren played together where we once did.

When the 2013 bush fires raged towards Dunalley a freak wind shift sent flames down the hill above Connellys and destroyed my beautiful brick home. A shed next door to me exploded and sent flames into an upstairs window. I sat on the beach with my cat in his cage and a box containing important papers and watched everything I owned being destroyed. Of course I rebuilt as I couldn't imagine wanting to live anywhere else but it has taken a long time to feel at home in the new house and I will always miss the things I lost; photos, paintings, books and even some special items of clothing.

Despite the loss of my home this is the only place I want to be. It is now no longer as isolated as it once was. When we were children it seemed to take forever to make the trip down here. Throughout the decades the highway has been widened and many of the bends have been removed. The road from the turnoff, which was once only gravelled, has now been sealed. Of course modern cars are also better and faster and the trip now takes me approximately forty minutes.

The view from the top of the hill is unchanged and is still a magical sight. It never fails to lift my heart when I round the bend and see it after being away from home, and I remember how, so long ago, we kids ran up the hill to be the first to see this view.

Biography – Barbara Knight

After many years as a teacher, housewife and mother I completed a Bachelor of Arts at UTAS, majoring in English Literature and History in the 1970s. I followed this with a graduate Diploma in Librarianship and worked in public libraries for sixteen years before my retirement.

During retirement I spent several years attempting to become partially self-sufficient by fishing and growing a huge variety of vegetables and fruits before turning to the more cerebral pursuits of writing and painting.

I am an avid reader, a long term member of book discussion groups and have been writing seriously for many years. I have had six short stories published in anthologies or magazines. I have also written a number of novels and a memoir.

www.ingramcontent.com/pod-product-compliance
Lightning Source LLC
Chambersburg PA
CBHW070257010526
44107CB00056B/2485